KNOW YOUR WALKING
&
CAMPING KIT

BY DARREN HARRIDENCE

THORNHILL PRESS LTD

FIRST PUBLISHED BY THORNHILL PRESS (1994)
PARKEND, GLOUCESTERSHIRE.

© DARREN HARRIDENCE 1994

ALL RIGHTS RESERVED. NO PART OF THIS PUBLICATION
MAY BE REPRODUCED, IN ANY FORM OR BY ANY MEANS,
EXCEPT FOR REVIEW, WITHOUT WRITTEN PERMISSION
FROM THE PUBLISHER.

ISBN 0 946328 55 2

PRINTED IN GREAT BRITAIN BY HILLMAN PRINTERS
(FROME) LTD, FROME, SOMERSET

What's the use of worrying ?
It never was worth while,
so, pack up your troubles in your old kit-bag,
And smile, smile, smile.

> George Asaf (George H. Powell)
> Pack up your troubles in your old kit bag. (1915).

Thanks to Steven, Anne & Peter Caldwell
for checking part of the manuscript

CONTENTS

	PAGE
INTRODUCTION....................................	5
1. BOOTS:..	9
Boot fit	42
2. WATERPROOFS..............................	48
3. RUCKSACKS:..................................	66
Daysacks.......................................	80
4. GENERAL CLOTHING:....................	85
Fleece...	91
Thermals.......................................	98
Socks..	104
5. SLEEPING BAGS..............................	111
6. ROLL MATS....................................	133
7. STOVES..	139
8. TENTS...	147

Introduction.

To what do we owe the tremendous popularity of our countryside? There could be many influences, including the war, the scouts, even the hippy movement. For campers - the relative cheapness of the camping holiday and for walkers, the relative modern ease of reaching the countryside. Perhaps the increase in outdoor activities has benefited from the keep fit awareness era, the green movement or simply our increase in leisure time. Let us not overlook the obvious pleasures in landscape beauties and stepping closer to nature, but unquestionably, the main motive for most of us is the desire to escape our regular daily environment.

Even so, with a chicken and egg situation, it is also fair to note that part of the growing success and love for the great outdoors owes its existence to the vastly improved comfort levels achieved by the introduction of better and better walking and camping kit.

The camping, and thus, walking equipment revolution truly began during the mid seventies, with the emphasis towards lightweight products. No longer would outdoor enthusiasts have to challenge the British weather armed only with army surplus cast - offs and all manner of adapted domestic gear.

Designs, aided by technology, leaped on through the early eighties before inevitably petering out towards a more steady evolution. Fewer new products and designs now appear each year, but none the less are still improving. During this time, encouraged by a new fitness-aware public, walking superseded angling as the fastest growing outdoor leisure activity.

Today, walking and camping are big business. With any amount of manufacturers bartering for shop shelf space, the choice of kit available from so many competitors has become confusing, unnecessary, ridiculous and almost impossible.

It seems that as the list of redeveloped, revitalized, new and improved products designed for the walker/camper increases, the appetite and the interest of the walking public still faithfully keeps pace. Perhaps this is testimony to the manufacturers themselves and one good reason why a new annual product range is maintained.

The quest for knowledge about new products and improved designs holds a wealth of interest for many walkers. For many of us, the interest in the equipment we use is a happy extension of the activity.

Some walkers can find the task of buying a new day-sack, for example, an irritating chore, but for others, an interesting exercise in research, budgeting, critical analysis and decision making. The amount of choice in all spheres of "walker's" equipment, creates a very competitive market and it appears that one way to argue that your product is a better choice than your competitors is to describe and explain your (hopefully) superior design in greater detail.

With such a high level of product knowledge available, we consumers can, as a result, only feel obliged to take careful interest in such issues as moisture vapour transmission rates, fabric osmotic balance, hydrophilic and hydrophobic systems, hydrostatic head measurements, etc etc! I know of no other industry where the end user is invited to such dizzying standards of design knowledge.

With such detail now available it's surprising that so much misunderstanding can still exist. Most oddly, misunderstandings don't emerge from the complex details but usually from the product's basic ideals and objectives.

The mass competition and heavy publicity as to why one product is technically better than another, might have made the consumer confused about which is best, but at least the consumer can be sure about one thing; if there's an argument over which one might be better, then there is definitely one that is worse. It's the fear of being saddled with that product that perhaps dominates the modern purchaser's priorities most of all.

Am I being too critical in writing this book? I prefer to think that I'm helping to make the best of a bad lot, an attempt at sorting out the mess.

On writing it, I was actually surprised not by the amount I had to say, but more by the amount I had to omit. (A whole book could be dedicated to boots alone), maybe as a thoughtful gesture to the rain forests but mainly due to what I felt was unnecessary to include. I've tried to cover most products with more detail than most other reads, but have only become excessive where I felt it was harmless.

This is not a "how to" book and isn't intended primarily as a buyer's guide. This book tries to cater for the growing demand for clearer knowledge from potential, or regular, users.

You'll notice how I refrain from deliberating over specific brands and product models as this is your job, but made easier, with the information in this book. It would also date this material within months! At the very least, the book should help you to understand your equipment and increase your awareness of what's available.

The book looks at the major items of kit, as smaller items (e.g, water bottles) rely upon common sense. The information caters for walkers (rambling, hill/fell walking, scrambling, etc) and modern campers or backpackers. (Not traditional family camping).

Throughout I've tried to avoid stating the completely obvious, while not shunning novices. Hopefully I've provided a more in-depth attitude not usually applied to such subjects.

I've tried, as often as possible, to remain a cold and callous reporter of the facts, only adding my penny's worth where I have felt it necessary, and have included a few notes and details which may be of passing interest to users.

Another British trade show has passed and new ranges are poised for launch, and yes, it's still true, someone, somewhere has faithfully managed yet again to think of something new.

aWainwright™
"THE MASTER FELLWALKER"
by K

One piece leather upper made from the best water resistant Pittards WR100 leather.

Foam padded leather bellows tongue and ankle cuff.

The boot is lined with CAMBRELLE® bonded to a water-proofing membrane.

Dual density, lightweight and resilient sole.

Stitched with an 'anti-wick' water resistant thread.

Removable and washable footbed, moulded to the contour of your foot.

D-rings and Ski hooks have been coated to resist rusting.

Rubber foxing protects against scrapes on rough terrain.

Alfred Wainwright has inspired thousands of walkers. During his lifetime he brought the joys of fellwalking to the public through his diaries, notes and sketches. He became known as The Master Fellwalker.

K Shoes have been making footwear in the English Lake District since 1842. The original walking boots were made for shepherds walking over 40 miles a day.

The Wainwright boot by K Shoes is the classic lightweight boot, designed to the highest standards, combining the Wainwright values of walking heritage with quality, craftsmanship and technology.

*For details of stockists contact:
Karen Abbott, Customer Service Dept
K Shoes, Kendal, Cumbria LA9 7BT
Tel: 0539 724343

K SHOES

BY APPOINTMENT TO H.M. THE QUEEN
BOOTMAKERS

BY APPOINTMENT TO H.M. QUEEN ELIZABETH
THE QUEEN MOTHER
BOOTMAKERS

BOOTS.

Since the first leisure excursions headed for the hills, walking boots have always remained the most personalised piece of a walker's kit. Of all the general pieces of equipment a walker may collect, no other seems to become as personal, unique, as private as the old pair of boots. Perhaps it's because they are the only item still made from natural material; perhaps because no two pairs of used boots look the same. For that matter, no two pairs of walking boots quite feel the same. As with cars, boots can seemingly produce Monday morning and Friday afternoon pairs. An experienced mountaineer may handle his old and trusty ice axe with fond sentimentality, but for the rest of us, walking boots are the closest thing to any part of our walking wardrobe that holds any form of regret and melancholy when, alas, their travelling days are over.

For those of you who have had nothing but unimpressive, even painful, experiences with walking boots, then do take a, however sceptical, look at the "Boot Fit" section (page 41), as no written word about choosing walking boots should be complete without reference to the correct fitting.

When Albert F. Mummery replaced his hob nailed boots for the particularly difficult parts of the first ascent of the Grepon (Chamonix-France) in 1881, with his rubber soled plimsoles for most probably the first time by any climber, his friends thought him mad; until his climbing improved and his technique appeared easier.

Italian walker, Vitale Bramani, dissatisfied with his leather-soled boots, also believed in the use of rubber as an outer sole. In 1937, due to the improved grip and traction rubber would give him over rocks and hard ground, he designed and invented the first purpose-made rubber sole for hill walking and climbing. Originally a hobnailed rubber sole, over the years it would quickly evolve into the classic commando sole (Lugged, Montagna) displaying its familiar tread pattern, which still enjoys popular use on many of today's walking and industrial boots. These soles, proudly displaying their brand name of Vibram (named after it's owner/creator) gave birth to hundreds of imitations. That particular tread pattern would set the standard for all other outdoor soles and barely modified, would still comfortably sell within today's competitive market. Trails of white scratches etching their way across the rocks of mountains, left behind by the sole-protecting nails of hob-nailed boots, have long since been smoothed away.

Actually, hob-nailed boots could be considered better performers over nearly all types of terrain except rock, (Although they did make a bit of a mess of grassy slopes and paths). The lugged rubber soles' vastly superior performance over rock however, and just about satisfactory enough capabilities over other surfaces, scored an overall win.

This initial Italian dominance would return by the nineteen eighties, not only with rubber soles, but in the manufacture of entire climbing and walking boots. Many would now argue that the Italians are the best producers of quality leather goods in the world. How great the growth from the humble origins of their original footwear industry!

Way back, during the eighteen fifties, the cobblers of Montebelluna would cater for the locals who, each Wednesday, headed into town for their weekly shopping. These would present the first opportunity for the shoe makers to offer and sell their "Dalamre" boots; ugly, but certainly strong and practical.

Although until recently, the Bulgarians (plus Czechoslavakia) sold the highest quantity of walking boots globally, it is the Italians who, at least in the Japanese, U.K, and home markets, boast the largest boot sales, (Leather boots aren't so popular in America and the rest of Europe).

Of the more experienced walkers who visit a walking shop, common coments concerning boots revolve around how the boots have changed. Boots changed considerably through the eighties and today rarely reflect their traditional pre-lightweight days. The biggest radical shake-up in the boot design arrived at the beginning of the eighties in the form of the Treklite. This boot, by the Italian company Zamberlan, first questioned and then proved that to achieve a comfortable and well performing boot you need not rely on the traditional and unchallenged methods of boot design. Hefty weights were unnecessary, chunky soles were not needed, soft leathers could be used and, most notably, heavy stiff shanks (along with all their inherent problems) could be discarded. To quote the makers, this boot became the benchmark of future boot design.

Also around this time, fabric boots first appeared, in the form of the Karrimor K.S.B, and promised a whole new era in lightweight fabric designs. This first popular fabric phase, however, soon faded away, following the many problems with achieving a watertight finish. It seemed that while some customers were totally satisfied with their pair, many others weren't. The subsequently discontinued K.S.B would have to wait another ten years before being reintroduced, latching onto a new growing fabric era, but only once waterproof fabric technology had been improved substantially enough to avoid previous problems.

Through the eighties, from time to time, fabric boots enjoyed a slight re-emergence, leading to the general opinion that sales of fabric boots performed like economy; up and down. But in the early nineties it seems that, with lessons learnt, fabric boots have genuinely emerged once again and look set to maintain, perhaps increase, their U.K boot market's share. Along with design improvements and trekking holidays abroad, in warmer, dryer climates, the apparent improvement of British summers, have contributed to their second wind.

Of all the areas of a walker's kit, none seems to create as many experts and as much confused caution and concern as walking boots.

CHOOSING BOOTS; A continued introduction including advice and information on choosing boots.

Homing in on the dearest options isn't the safest way of finding the best boots. Only up in the quality end of proceedings can boots arguably claim to be designed for specific styles of use. Choosing the dearest boot will usually land you with a winter boot, not necessarily what you require. As most boots are for general purpose use, one effective method of rationalising a selection is simply asking yourself what kind of budget you have in mind. If somebody asks me for a boot to suggest and recommend, and their budget is fifty pounds, then I recommend the fifty pound boot. If they don't fit or aren't quite comfortable then we mill around that area of the range; but it's given us direction, a starting point. None of these general purpose boots are anti any particular landscape.

You need a strategy, i.e. a budget range. Set yourself a few points that you require, some specifications that sound attractive. Describe the boot that you require to yourself, if not to the shop assistant. Simply asking for something lightweight doesn't help much these days. Heavy boots are virtually extinct. Unfortunately there are many boot shoppers around who know exactly what they don't want, but haven't a clue what they do want.

There are no other great secrets. Usually by coincidence some boots are more suitable for certain types of walking than others, but all tend to overlap. Many voices might try to categorise boots by seasons but the vast majority are for general purpose use. Angles of hills at three thousand feet can be the same as at only two feet above sea level. Stones are just as hard along canal tow paths as at the top of Ben Nevis. (Some people may describe boot strengths as, e.g, "a medium to stiff boot". Make of this what you can. If you're a high-level fellwalker with a mid-level budget, then manufacturer's references to which are for what, are all irrelevant anyway. Usually referring to a leather boot as two season, or summer season, simply means, "the cheaper option". It sounds far better than the "not so good boot".

Potential customers should bear in mind that with modern boots they are paying for comfort and performance, not their life expectancy. Boots, unfortunately, rarely last as long as many people might hope and shouldn't be related to traditional boots.

A good walking shop will be only too pleased to allow you to return a pair of boots after a few days if you're not entirely sure about them, provided you haven't worn them outside. You might be able to arrange with the shop, leaving two suitable cheques and taking two pairs of boots, to deliberate over, for only a couple of days, in your own time at home. Once you've made your choice, the shop keeper returns one of your cheques with the return of the rejected pair of boots.

Besides comfort, what are the points you should look out for when selecting boots? Hopefully most will have become apparent throughout this collective chapter concentrating on the design features of boots, but a few simple points can quickly tell a good from bad...

A lot of people armed with a little walking boot knowledge have been issued with the brief of pursuing boots with a one piece leather upper (No side seam). Usually the cheaper boots display side seams, described as two-piece leather uppers. (Some boots are referred to as half piece uppers, as they only use a single seam on the inner side of the foot. Some fabric boots also use one piece suede uppers). The main problem with seams lies in the addition of extra stitching holes with the likelihood of water seeping inside. (Some manufacturers use non-wicking thread). Occasionally seams are secured with a double row of stitching which helps strengthen the joint, but naturally can increase even further the chances of water seepage.

One piece leather uppers make a perfectly valid point and one to bear in mind, but unfortunately they are often promoted in importance, far above more immediate concerns on the list of boot priorities. There are many examples of two-piece leather walking boots costing the same as one piece leather uppers, but sometimes, because the two-piece version has nice anti-lateral twist, a spring to the toe, genuine anatomical footbed, sound supporting and subtle shaping to its style and leather (explanations to follow), means, although it hasn't the one piece upper, it is still a far better boot. One-piece leather uppers are a desirable feature but should only draw attention after a number of other criteria have met.

One of the most important parts of a good walking boot (often underestimated) is its midsole. Pick up a walking boot and try to twist its sole. Do not flex its length, but force the toe end to twist in opposite direction to its heel end. (This tests its longitudinal torsion). A good boot will offer good resistance to this, yet still flex comfortably in length. (Although boots that might feel too firm are often better once your entire body weight is upon them. Don't bend boots by pinching the toes. Boots will soften with use). It's this resistance to lateral twist, across the forefoot, that offers the greatest area of support.

When the length is flexed the sole should energetically spring back into shape, unlike some with a rather lethargic reshaping. Usually midsoles made from nylon create a curve when flexed; preferable to some that tend eventually to end up creasing along the point of flex.

Press, with a strong thumb, the middle of the forefoot area to discover if there's enough strength and firmness to protect you from the uncomfortable feeling of stones.

Generally, the heavier you are, the stiffer the boot you should adopt. If you participate in hundred mile walks and clock up thousands of kilometres each year, then you should require a stronger boot, even if only to help compensate for the boot's fast reduction in flex strength. Backpackers carrying heavier weight might also consider something more substantial.

Traditionally, when shopping for boots, there are a handful of classic points to look out for, which at one time had to be covered in great detail, as they were still highly relevant. Fortunately these features to avoid are now either superseded or improved. Reference to making sure the boots have a stitched-in tongue (bellows tongue), screwed on soles, real leather linings, metal hooks instead of punched holes, good thick tread and stainless steel shanks (less likely to rust), to recall a few, are now unnecessary.

FABRIC BOOTS. (Introduction)

Usually made from a mixture of nylon fabric and suede, fabric boots offer a popular alternative to traditional leather options. The general understanding is that fabric boots are not only cooler, but also provide softer (no breaking in), more comfortable performance. This is commonly the case, but usually relates to the poorer versions, which provide little support or genuine comfort in use.

It seems that the majority of all fabric boot sales stem from many people's steadfast belief that all leather walking boots are heavy, stiff and horrible. These days, this is rarely just. Such suspicions are usually founded simply on appearances. Unfortunately, people often apply assumed knowledge to the weights of both leather and fabric boots.

Boots

Reality reminds us that if a fabric boot is to offer as much support and protection as an average modern leather boot, then it needs to be of exactly equal weight. The midsoles need to be the same. Stones don't become soft at the sight of fabric boots. A fabric boot that doesn't offer the same support and genuine comfort as a decent leather alternative, isn't an alternative, but an inferior boot.

The one indisputable advantage all fabric boots offer is better 'breathability'. Due to larger holes in the weave of nylon fabrics, compared to leather, they provide cooler performance in hot weather and warmer climates. As a result, they are the only strain of boot that merits the invention of the terms (for boots) two, or summer, season.

Unfortunately, this creates their main disadvantage. They are not waterproof. (Sprays, etc, can help combat the problem, but never convincingly). As a result they are only suitable as summer or dry climate boots. However...

To overcome their lack of waterproofing (limited seasonal use) many fabric boots now incorporate additional waterproof linings. (Similar to a watertight sock anchored inside). Such linings should also be breathable, or your feet would still become damp due to their own perspiration. These are the only reasons boots use such liners, and customers should not become confused by the suggestion that they feature improved breathability over boots without similar linings. (i.e, an identical boot, without a waterproof liner, will breathe better than one with a waterproof/breathable lining).

More details in "WATERPROOF?" Page 36)

A fabric boot, with a waterproof liner, compared with an equally priced leather boot (without liner), will rarely offer equal quality or raw boot value, as such linings absorb much of the boot's cost.

Fabric boots have relatively low life expectancy. (I've found, on average, 18-24 months).

WINTER BOOTS. (Introduction)

Winter boots are usually, as their name suggests, only worn for winter

15

conditions, although there is an unusual breed of walkers who prefer the nearly rigid flex all year round. 'Winter conditions' (i.e, snow clad and frozen footpaths, usually in more mountainous regions) is the correct point to remember here, as some walkers have requested winter boots simply because they are going for a walk on Boxing day. Relatively great monsters of boots, with chunkier soles, thicker leathers and high solid ankle-support compared with traditional versions are still much lighter and improved. The main distinguishing feature is a thin but wide rubber rand that runs fully around the boot's lower edge, just above the sole. (This aids the grip of metal crampons and offers protection from abrasive ice).

Winter boots range from the totally rigid to the nearly rigid and include full leather or totally plastic constructions. Totally stiff/rigid boots are more suited to climbers of frozen waterfalls, etc. Boots with a slight flex, after extended use, suit the more modest, but still skilled, winter walker. With the aid of flexible walking crampons (occasionally a walking axe) such boots sport the strength necessary to enjoy various routes all year round, but are likely to become treacherous and dangerous when covered with snow and ice.

The main reasons winter boots sport a very stiff flex are: Repeatedly kicking steps, an important requirement for progressing up snow covered slopes and paths; Stiff boots help to keep crampons (metal spikes for soles), tied on with straps, safely secured; straps pulled tightly, on boots with soft uppers, can stem the foot's circulation; important to avoid in cold winter temperatures; Crampons, having to be solid, would come off boots that flex too greatly. (They may also snap).

Many a walker has tried using one pair of boots to suit both winter and general walking jobs. Unfortunately, the out-come is never very satisfactory. One reasonably stiff pair compromises summer comfort and winter performance = double compromise. Annoyingly the best and really only solution is two pairs. At the least, opt for stiffer boots, better for the winter and a bit of a pain in the summer, but never the opposite. People often ask, "I've got a such and such pair of boots, will they be able to take crampons?" My reply is that carpet slippers can take crampons but it all depends on the degree of success. The more flexible the boot, the more often you have to stop to restrap your crampons and for climbers, not using boots up to satisfactory strength may simply mean the quicker you fall off!

(Plastic boots usually accommodate step-in crampons - similar to snap-on ski bindings - but a few leather varieties now also offer the facility).

Plastic winter boots, as well as having features unique to themselves, resemble a clip ski boot in many ways, including the thick pullout liner. (A good ski shop, with special expertise in fitting and adjusting ski boots can also personalise plastic winter boots). Winter climbers who use them, swear by them, but they do require the mastering of a slightly new style of walking.

LADIES' BOOTS. (Introduction)

Designed specifically for a classically shaped lady's foot, ladies boots have proved highly successful and provide brilliantly improved comfort for many women. Differences include; Slightly easier flexing, slimmer lasts (foot shape), at the forefoot and the narrowing of the heel. Essentially a "lady's boot" accommodates slim feet. Loosely translated, lady's = slim. Unfortunately, simply because it states your sex as female on your birth certificate doesn't necessarily mean that these boots are going to be any better for you. Lady's boots are marvellous for providing slim fittings for women with slim feet. If you fancy a boot with a softer flex don't simply go for Ladies' boots a couple of sizes bigger as a solution. Other, softer, unisex models usually appeal to most women given the choice.

"Why won't these ladies' boots fit me?"

A NEW STYLE (Introduction)

'Snub-toed boots' is a nick-name I've given to a new style of walking boots that has emerged in recent years. They're easy to spot, for as the nick-name suggests, they appear to have snub toes; a blunt rounded toe shape with a particularly high lift, roll, or upturn to them. They're usually made of soft lightweight leathers, use lightweight shock-absorbing soles and have a cuff that's cut away at an unusually steep angle at the back. These lightweights are often found by many to be amongst the most comfortable of all boots, contrary to their stocky, clumsy, appearance. People often are puzzled about their design intent, but basically they simply offer an alternative boot shape and style. Whether you find them a better fit, or just prefer the look, there is nothing radically new in performance unless you count the improved comfort many shout about. Generally they all tend to suit more low-land uses.

VEGANS.

Boots for vegans, made purely from synthetic materials, have never taken off as well as people had once predicted. It seems that many manufacturers have introduced a totally synthetic boot only to drop it again the following season due to low demand.

Forever popular, not only with vegans, but also with many dry feet fans, are a brand of rubber boot. Made entirely from rubber and using a soft, moisture-absorbing lining, these popular half wellies, half boots, certainly seem to solve a lot of problems and keep many feet dry. Disadvantages include their heavy weight, lack of molding to shape and lack of breathability = Possibly hot in the summer, and damp and cold in the winter. Not used for anything too strenuous, but great for dog walking!

COMPONENTS OF BOOTS...

(Note: There are many technical names for specific areas describing

Boots

footwear, but here we shall use the common and universal descriptions for mapping boots.)

SOLES.

The choice and range of different soles available for walking boots is simply vast. Manufacturers of boots must select their soles (usually made by independent manufacturers) carefully by weighing up performance against cost. Displaying one of the well respected and known brands, is a true brownie point in winning over many potential customers.

Looking at the dazzling array of varying sole patterns and designs, quickly highlights differences in opinion as to what is deemed the best style of tread. (Most are now designed with computers). Recognizable brand logos and trademarks, depict the more respected and popular designs, particularly at the dearer end of affairs. Some designs seem to copy others. Others appear more radical. One recent style features traction facing forwards and backwards, supposedly providing reverse, as well as traditional forward grip.

While many still adopt the classic, definitive appearance of the commando sole, many have evolved a new philosophy in tread design. Deeply lugged soles reach through mud and wear well, but can be prone to balling up with mud, offering no grip. By widening the lugs (raised parts), shallowing the tread and smoothing away the heel instep (or heel breast), mud finds it considerably harder to cling on = more constant performance, although appearing less impressive in appearance. (+ spreading the load over a larger area with more sole in contact with the ground = improved traction). The "Supergrip" sole, by Vibram designed by "Klets" was the first to appear this way. Note; Cheaper soles with deeper tread than dearer shallower soles, won't necessarily last longer. It all depends upon the quality of rubber used. (More to follow).

The recent environmentally friendly world has stimulated the introduction, and increased presence of eco soles. (Designed to carry away less earth. e.g, from the tops of mountains and eroding footpaths). As the boots bend, lifting up soil with them as they go, the thoughtful tread patten allows the earth to fall back into its original place.

(Talking of the environment, when are we going to see soles that are made from recycled materials?)

Prominent square blocks on the toes and heels of some winter boots are used and required for step-in crampons.

Some modern sole designs incorporate a small rand around their top rim, almost cupping the uppers, not like a traditional, inch tall, additional rand, but a small feature sitting about three millimetres high. This thoughtful detail helps seal the edge of the boot, where leather and sole join, often an area prone to water seepage.

The varying compounds and mixture (including P.V.C and P.U) used in rubber soles all have varying performance characteristics (relating to cost, grip, durability, weight). Soles with a high carbon and/or neoprene content, produce a harder and more robust finish. (Less = malleable, rubbery texture, with improved grip). Concern about the many different types of sole mixtures, is for many, totally superfluous and for others, the better manufacturers will have chosen the better soles on your behalf anyway.

Shock absorbing soles: Relatively recent and certainly welcome. Many traditional solid soles have been superseded with less durable, but lighter and more comfortable alternatives.

Soles marrying different density materials together, (two or more layers glued together) combining hard compounds for the underside and soft*, shock absorbing, materials for uppers, are now a common sight on particularly lightweight boots (usually on fabric boots), as they improve on comfort and reduce weight.

(* A variety of materials but usually a form of enthylene vinyl acetate (E.V.A), used to capture millions of tiny air bubbles. E.V.A usually loses around 25% of it's compressibility after 500 miles running, but longer for walking).

Some choices of material can wick moisture up through the bottom of the boots, so some quality designs include a thin layer of solid rubber between the softer density material and the uppers.

Similar to trainer type soles, these soles are usually much firmer. A higher density is used to provide a more durable support. (Particularly

Boots

required if carrying a heavy pack). Unfortunately, drop an eye to some of the poorer fabric boots being worn and too often one side (usually the outer) of soft E.V.A sole unit/wedge has collapsed (crushed/condensed), leaving the user, usually unawares, to plod along super pronating. (A condition that can weaken ankles)

(Different colours often highlight layers of hard and soft. Built up at the rear with an extra slice = a die cut).

The other main alternative...

Dual density soles: = Stronger, tougher and much more durable. Usually found on dearer leather boots.

True versions are made from a single unit of rubber, but with two different densities present. At the very stage of moulding, the hard and soft densities are made to coexist alongside each other. High density = tougher, external tread. Lower density = softer shock-absorbing upper sections. Other advantages include; No risk of glued layers pulling apart. Even distribution = no collapsing. Reduction in weight over traditional counterparts.

(Soles with a dual density <u>tread pattern</u> are rare. Hard in the high wear areas, softer in others for improved grip)

There are many shock absorbing systems. E.g, particularly on winter boots, pieces of known shock absorbing compounds are clearly inserted into the heel region of a sole. (Many removable and replacement footbeds also offer shock absorption. See "Footbeds")

HEELS.

Again there are numerous designs to encounter, but all usually fall into one of four categories:

1. Traditional square block, (or steeped heel). Advantages; Durable and sure, digging-in grip when walking down hill. Disadvantages; Uncomfortable jarring action when walking the flats, (e.g, roads). Due to their right-angled square design, as your heel hits the ground to roll

forward and take the weight on that leg, they tend to slap the foot down in one quick brutal movement. There's no gradual transition of the load onto the forefoot. This can be very tiring. One solution...

2. Square heel with its heel-strike forward, (appearing from the side to have had a diagonal chunk sliced off the back). Advantage; With the strike ridge/point further forward, more directly under the ball of the foot, a much more comfortable rolling action is acquired. (Some such heel-strikes, from below, may appear horse-shoe shaped)

Disadvantages; When descending a hill, the heel mirrors the angle of the gradient, taking away the digging grip that the standard square heel offers. In recent years this has been held responsible for the tragic deaths of some hill walkers in, our more mountainous regions. The lack of down hill grip is evident, but unfair. Discussions with some of the world's leading mountaineers confirm that the heel shouldn't ideally be used for descending anyway, (unless fell running/scrambling). Your weight should be spread over the entire foot and sole (flat footed). With this correct method, these soles shouldn't give you any problems. If necessary, use the outside edge of the soles, descending in a zigzag pattern.

3. Many smaller heel-strikes forming a rounded curve. Advantages; Heel-strike spread over a much larger area, helping to roll the foot down, creating a gradual transition with no sudden shift of weight; but still with channels and chunks, providing the grip of many smaller square heels.

Disadvantages; Many satisfied users, but style is accused of being slightly too aggressive and perhaps damaging to the environment. Careful inspection should be made regularly to the wear and tear of the important heel tread. Tread may clog up with mud.

4. Square heel with shock absorption, (usually, not an exact right angled heel, but satisfactory).

Advantages; Effective square heel grip + shock absorption to reduce traditional jarring effects. Often considered the most satisfactory solution. (Some versions of heel number 3 now also feature additional shock absorption).

MIDSOLES.

(Before we proceed, there is often confusion caused by correct or incorrect names that relate both to traditional and modern components. Even in recent history, midsoles have confused meanings. Here we use the new, current and general understandings).

Lasts and shanks generally no longer exist in walking boots. (Steel shanks are still reasonably common in cheaper fabric boots). A "last" was a form of template dictating the shape and fit of footwear and was the main anchoring point for all the other ingredients that made up a boot. The shank provided stiffness = support, taking most of the strain off the arch and stopping the boot and foot from twisting.

Resembling a metal ruler, running the boot's inner length between sole and upper last, shanks were usually steel and had the advantage of not rotting and splitting as wooden shanks might. Disadvantages included; rusting (stainless steel versions reduce this), extra weight and often eventual snapping. Half and three-quarter length shanks are sometimes used; allowing only the forefoot area to flex.

Main disadvantage with shanks (and traditional boots): A twelve inch metal ruler bends easier than a four inch ruler = larger and smaller boots didn't have proportionate stiffness. Larger feet usually carry more weight, ironically leaving smaller-footed and lighter people with the stiffer boots.

What changed all this and made boots considerably lighter, was the advent of the nylon midsole (or synthetic shank). Instead of using a last (usually made from a thick leather slab), and a shank to do two jobs, the midsole would encompass both duties. Effectively a much stronger last, made from solid nylon (or injected polypropylene, and layers of polyethylene) it was light, rust proof and most of all could be moulded (stamped out or sometimes injection moulded) to provide each and every size and boot model with its own unique degree of strength and flex. It is this that now provides the core nucleus for most modern walking boots. (Alternatives include; fibreglass, celtex, texon. The use of metal frames and varying types of nylons sandwiched together, creating a longer life). From inside the boot pull out the loose footbed resting inside to see the midsole clearly. Along with the quality and condition of the boot uppers, it's this component that usually dictates whether a boot is worth resoling or not, depending upon how much strength remains, as midsoles soften with use.

Modern midsoles provide: Underfoot protection, e.g, reducing the feeling of stones. Support, e.g, preventing soles twisting when walking across the side of a hill.

Following this new design logic, cheaper midsoles have appeared using all sorts of materials. Some are better than others, some are very poor, tending to crease rather than bend. Others have a nasty habit of absorbing moisture, being from what comes very close to reconstituted cardboard. (Compact midsoles = hardboard).

It's this area of boot construction that usually goes undetected by too many novice boot shoppers.

In the traditional sense of the phrase, mainly due to modern midsoles, boots no longer need to be "broken in". These days you can go off marching in new boots straight away, but a genuine improvement in comfort and flex will often prevail after approximately 30-40 miles. "Breaking in" traditionally refers to simply getting boots to bend. Most modern boots are like new shoes, merely requiring softening up. (There is much advice and many differing methods suggested for softening up boots, but the simplest and best is use. Walk in them. Shorter walks at first, then gradually increase them according to your confidence in their improving comfort). Stories of walking up streams, etc, may have been relevant for wooden shanks, but not nylon midsoles. Some waxes can soften leathers, but abide by instructions; too much of some can cause damage.

Common in some E.V.A sole units, midsoles help spread weight evenly over the entire sole. Plastic heel counters (usually thermo-plastic) perform a similar job (+ correcting heel stance) but many travel further down the boot, also helping to create a water stopping type of rand, (sometimes known as a seawall rand). With curved heights and shallows, they also help dictate where the leather creases and boots flex.

Coinciding with moulded midsoles, a slight lift at the mid forefoot of the sole, could be introduced, creating a natural roll and anatomic flex line. (With steel shanks, your feet had to dictate where the boots flexed) This natural curve may be prominent on a hard shop floor, but it is less obvious once on grass and uneven ground. This increased "spring" in the sole seems almost to do the walking for you. Foot flexes less = reduced heel movement and arches becoming less tired = improved overall comfort.

ATTACHING SOLE AND MIDSOLE TO UPPERS.

The vast majority of boots, soles and midsoles are simply glued (bonded) together; coincidentally providing advantages in cost, weight and resoling. Sometimes known as scatola. (Thin base coverings on some nylon midsoles improve sole adhesion). Reasonably rare, a slight variation on gluing is to use molten neoprene, injected under pressure.

Along with glueing (sometimes referred to as cementing) vulcanising is another common method among the cheap budget boots. (Sole bonded to upper using a mixture of pressure and heat). For a lot of boots and users, it does the job.

(Small tacks may still be used, as glue dries).

However, while glueing science is more than perfectly adequate for most people's needs, occasionally a stronger more reliable method is required; e.g, winter boots, persistent scrambling over rocks, anyone who might be thousands of miles from home. Traditional systems have included screwed, glued and sewn examples, (sometimes all three) but with stronger modern glues, only the addition of stitching (usually blake stitching) is necessary.

On common bonded constructions (glued) the edge of the leather upper folds down underneath the midsole and is sandwiched, along with the glue, between the midsole and the rubber outer sole. Boots that are also blake sewn (or inside stitched) have a hidden line of stitching around the midsole's circumference, threading through into the leather lip that folds under the midsole's edge.

Just about still available, although less watertight, are traditionally welted soles. (Sometimes called Norwegian welts). This is when a thick line (or more) of stitching is clearly visible around the outside edge of the boot, creating a thin ledge where the leather doesn't turn inside, but outside, revealing it's edge and thickness. (Usually found on traditionally styled shanked boots). The stitching simply punches through this leather lip and into the sole, (or last, or trad-midsole, which is bonded to the rubber outer sole) pinching the two/three together. Once the most common method used, this style is now only found on either the most consciously traditional of boots, catering for a tiny and decreasing market, or on traditional winter boots. Some of these winter boots, again consciously styled, also offer this welted style because edging is believed, by some, to be easier. (Edging = e.g, walking along a thin lip of rock with only the boot's edge in contact). The main advantage this European welting system had over other, now extinct, versions (in Britain) was an improved final fit, as the last was, uniquely added early on in the construction stages.

Many E.V.A wedged soles are tension lasted. (Glued/bonded under tension, achieving a curved shape). Poorer sole units are cut/trimmed before fitting = smooth edges, but usually too much tension = bowing walls, poor curve, weaker durability. Trimmed once glued, usually = rougher finish, but better quality shaping and improved durability.

UPPERS.

Leather: In Britain, leather is still the most common material used for walking boot uppers. The different grades of quality all relate to many factors. Including: Different parts of the creature's anatomy. Different types of treatment during tanning. Different uses for waste and scraps. Different methods of making more substantial, wafer thin leathers.

Still the best and most suitable choice for tough footwear, it combines comfort, breathability, weather resistance, durability and relative cheapness.

Boots

Gone are the days when most boots used stiff and heavy leather supplied by mature creatures, probably the knacker's yard. Today, inspired by the Italians, calf leather is the order of the day. (Soft young leathers). Black and dark brown boots have mostly disappeared making way for the continental light, orangy brown appearance. This colour (often sprayed on) now sends signals to our subconscious, suggesting that the leather must be soft and light. This is why most boots, including imposter leathers, now also appear in light brown tones.

Full grain calf (or Anfibio) leather is a term usually used to describe the best leathers of today's boots. The best quality examples used in general purpose and high level boots usually use thicker leathers, approximately 2.5mm gauge, with 3.mms found in winter boots. Full grain leather is the part used by the original owner, the animal, on the very outside. (Known in the leather trade as top grain)

Hides are sliced or split, as the majority of a hide is too thick to use in its natural state. Different layers are gained all providing different grades, (sometimes only split into two layers. The inner layer is often known as split leather) but the first outside layer is the best for walking boots. It's the toughest, most water repellent and waterproofable!

The various layers found deeper into animal's hide are suitable either for trimmings, inside linings, or often appearing as suede. True suede boots are soft, but difficult to proof properly and don't have nearly the same durability as the top grain (full grain) leather.

Often these top grain leathers were buffed up, to smooth away the animal's natural porous holes, leaving a uniform finish. (Known as smooth grain leather). But fashions change and with the invasion of poor, almost imitation leathers, customers appreciate being able to see the original animal grains. (Unbuffed leather is also thought to be slightly tougher)

Virtually all full grain leather boots (particularly on the British market) use it the way nature intended it, with it's smooth side outside. This leaves the softer finish (flesh side) protected on the inside. Is this necessarily the best way? If you've ever noticed that cows are waterproof, it's due to the constitution of a thin layer in the smooth side of full grain leather. To have this barrier layer on the outside, protecting all that's inside from the elements, is the most logical choice.

Losing the battle is the once common alternative, exposing the soft flesh side to the outside. The idea avoids utilising the thin water resistant barrier on the outside, where it's exposed to elements that may damage and penetrate it. (E.g, brambles and rocks scuffing the surface). By having this delicate barrier (smooth side) on the inside of the boot, its life is prolonged, helping to keep the wearer's feet dry. This choice of use, often wrongly confused with suede, now only usually appears on some American and northern European boots, or occasionally as pre-greased leather. Its down-sides include; the softer exterior slowly but persistently breaking down and wearing away, while also easily absorbing moisture, making the boots heavy.

(Rough hide appears similar to suede but is simply as the name describes).

Tanning: A hide that hasn't enjoyed various chemical processes, rots very quickly when exposed to water. This isn't a specific feature you should be looking for, but a standard procedure for all leathers. In it's raw state, animal skin is quite weak; when wet it quickly rots; when dry, it becomes brittle and stiff. Tanning makes the hide flexible, insoluble in water, resistant to decay and generally maintains it's malleable good health. Tanning also offers the potential to give leathers their own characteristics, whether hard and tough or soft and easily malleable.

Once unwanted materials were removed, leaving only the core derma, traditionally skins were tanned by a long series of soakings and dryings, using vegetable oils. (Oak bark provides particularly high levels of suitable tanning oils). But modern factory methods enroll the use of the dyeing drum (resembling a giant washing machine) which reduces pungent smells due to the use of more efficient mineral treatments. Splitting machines not only reduced hides to the required gauge but also reduce waste with their improved accuracy. Instead of a leather being hand thinned with sharp tools, a single hide is split, creating two from one.

Of mineral treatments, chromium salts are often used to create a dry, hard and shiny finish, but a few manufacturers still prefer to use leathers subjected to vegetable tanning as they tend to create a softer appearance. Various tools then give the hides the cosmetic shine.

Boots

The main interest to any modern boot is "pre-tanned leather"; leathers that boast an impregnation of water repellent properties. Nearly every range and brand of boot now includes leathers that have a treatment which claims to improve the leather's water resistance, or drying time. To help the leather absorb less moisture, (around only 30% of its own dry weight) it's soaked and treated with various substances, usually a silicon mixture. The many names describing the same product, but offered from different boot manufacturers, are all descriptive and similar. I find that these treated leathers do little to improve the waterproofness of boots in use, but do seem to improve their drying times and all are generally agreed to be much of a muchness. (Quicker drying times are particularly handy when away walking for a number of days or more. Pulling on damp boots of a morning is never nice). Unfortunately, the condition of these leathers with their low water absorptions does not last indefinitely. They tend to wear off, in order of key high flex areas, after about eighteen months of regular soakings.

There are some "leathers" that only just manage to claim the description. Reconstituted leather is often used for the more inexpensive of boots. Probably the most common method of producing economy priced leathers, is to continuously skim a large reconstituted block. This produces an almost wafer thin sheet of leather. Obviously the result is a weak one and requires the added strength of a clear P.U (polyurethane) or P.V.C. (acrylic and polyvinyl chloride). This can actually provide a highly water repellent result but of low breathability. Occasionally these coatings are stippled to create a full grain appearance, but they shouldn't fool any half experienced eye.

Many quality leathers are also P.U. coated, either to give them a slight water repellantly or just a shine on a shop shelf. Quality, but thin, lightweight leathers do require it's added durability.

Some boots appear with a greasy finish. This, "greased leather", is how many boots once appeared in the hope of improving water repellantly while always maintaining suppleness after continuous soakings and dryings. More often than not, modern examples (with reversed leather) are merely an aesthetic device, supposedly creating a fashionable or stylish image.

Synthetic uppers (Fabric boots): Fabrics (made from nylon for durability and unaffected response to water) are attractive to many as they, supposedly, offer a lighter and softer alternative to leather. The weave of a texturised nylon does provide improved breathability, particularly appreciated in hot climates, but suede is usually added at key, high wear, areas to provide extra strength. In fabric footwear, the combination of suede and nylon is as common as rubber tyres and metal wheels.

Where fabric meets suede, all quality boots should feature double rows of stitching.

The most prominent varying suede feature revolves around the toe. Sometimes suede is used to trim around the toe, but on stronger, more substantial boots, it encompasses the entire toe box.

People requiring the breathability of fabric but the strength of leather may be interested in the occasional pairing of fabric and leather, but the difference in life expectancies make this, for most, an illogical choice.

The most common of fabrics used in fabric productions incorporates Cordura. (Or similar, if only in appearance). Developed in the sixties by Du Pont, it's extremely durable, highly abrasion resistant and highly tear resistant, but it's heavy texture makes it difficult to proof. Used in all sorts of applications, such as rucksacks and gloves, it's most commonly found in 1000 denier weights (denier = thickness of textile fibres) which is a little too stiff for footwear, so usually a lighter 330 denier is used.

Both leather and fabric uppers are usually accompanied inside by many various man-made materials, all intended to add strength, shape and substance. Designed to help maintain the boot's shape, usually a plastic or latex is chosen. Kevlar has now been added to the list. (Occasionally, boots incorporate all-weather insulations such as Thermolite).

All boots (excluding some weak fabric versions) incorporate lightweight plastic protection from stones and maintain crucial fit. Such toe counters or caps are also important for kicking steps.

Many boot uppers also feature rands, (or foxing). Usually black and made from rubber, resembling a thick texturised rubber band, they skirt the bottom edge (just above the soles) of the boot. Their appearance has little to do with improving waterproof standards, but offer protection against scuffing. (Many travel internally far under the boot. Some create a cup for the uppers to sit in, which can provide extra lateral support). Common on winter boots, many quality lightweight general purpose boots now enroll their protection; particularly needed for the thinner leather uppers.

This area, on leather boots, needs to be scuffed/roughed up to aid the rand's adhesion, (with glue). The continuity of machines provide the best job, as hand finished versions may miss areas and lead to rands parting from their uppers. (But easily remedied with suitable glue).

FOOTBEDS. (Or in-soles)

One component of all modern boots, greatly improving comfort and fit, is the footbed. These are the sole sized and foot shaped removable liners that rest inside practically all modern boots. There are almost as many variations as there are boots, but all aim to serve the same purpose. By selecting and experimenting they can offer the facility of slightly personalising your boot's feel and comfort.

The most usual types are made from a very lightweight and reasonably firm solid foam, stamped out into a thin flexible mould, reflecting the bottom of an average foot. They raise the heel minutely and offer a little arch support. Covered in a thin layer of hard wearing, non-slip anti-odour material, they help reduce internal foot movement and avoid heat spots. Becoming less common is a variety that includes a very subtle bulge, living in the centre of the forefoot. This slight lift is intended to relieve general fatigue.

There are many pathetic versions available, but a little experience and common sense can quickly select the better performers. Most footbeds last many hundreds of miles, but replacements are cheap and effortless to fit.

Research has revealed that our bones (shins, knees, back and even

31

head) often suffer from impact shock as we walk, which in recent years has turned much attention towards the use of shock absorbing systems, either incorporated in the sole unit (and socks) or, increasingly, as an integral role for footbeds.

Various foams, including P.U.R and numerous rubber type compounds provide a bewildering selection. Most notable of all, with the highest profile, is a brand that produces a range of footbeds, displaying impact compounds in a distinctive red. They claim their product reduces, or absorbs, impact shock by up to 95% and owes it's effectiveness to absorbing and dissipating shock energy slowly. (This type of product is often relatively heavy, but lightweight versions, utilising impact areas in only key areas, are available).

Some footbeds have even claimed to provide additional protection against lateral, or twisting, tension along with promoting blood flow and helping to reduce fatigue. There are many highly imaginative solutions, incorporating sealed impact air chambers and the use of jelly pads or sacks.

Whether achieved by a machine in a shop or in the oven at home, memory footbeds are moulded from the sole of your feet, providing a personalised fit. By spreading the load evenly over a larger area of your feet, they distribute pressure and improve comfort, relieve muscles and help blood flow. However, in ski boots, where your foot shouldn't move, memory footbeds are great, but walking in walking boots is a different kettle of fish. Reasons why include:

1. Your feet are constantly moving and flexing as you walk; i.e, constantly changing shape. 2. As the footbeds bend, they too distort their shape, arguing with the shape of your feet. 3. Your feet expand and swell over walking periods = footbeds are no longer accurate.

If you do choose to try such footbeds and have them fitted at a shop, check that edges are trimmed properly. (Ideally on a ski grinder). Neatly finished, the angle of the edges should mirror and fit neatly against the inside of the boot. Messy edges can distort the footbed's shape. (Try them for severe foot problems, not as corrective medicine, but subtly, helping to make the best of a bad lot).

Footbeds that claim to offer warm feet, usually use some kind of thin

Boots

reflective metal. This might work in ski boots, but remains unconvincing in walking boots. (Try corrugated cardboard + not forgetting decent combinations of warm woollen socks).

TONGUE.

By using a bellows design, the tongue can be pulled out adequately far enough to allow a foot to slide in and out while also blocking water entry. The bellows (or galoshes) are the two pieces of thin leather (on leather boots) that fold down neatly on either side of the tongue. Proofed properly, they should be reasonably watertight, but are also effective at repelling small annoying stones. They should be tucked neatly and evenly down the sides of the boot and over your feet. In time they will rest there naturally, while also helping to spread the load of laces and improve comfort.

Many boots feature a hinged tongue. This is a short line, or tuck, of stitching that tailors the tongue slightly to coincide more readily with the top of your feet.

Some tongues may seem to dig in at the top of your feet, but this is one of the first areas of a boot to soften up, soon sitting comfortably.

Others include a couple of short vertical slits intended for laces to be threaded through and holding the tongue directly in place. Sceptics point out that such additions become prone to water leakage. Besides, the tongue should be allowed to settle where it's most naturally comfortable.

All tongues are now padded and often lined, most commonly with side, but occasionally with synthetic alternatives, apt at absorbing perspiration.

Walking shoes often adopt a tongue design which rests on the outside. (External tongue = prevents grit/pebbles entering).

LACES.

Even something as apparently simple as a boot-lace has its own share of differing qualities. Approximately 150cms long, boot laces are available in either flat or round forms. (Square also if you include leather laces, but these, even though giving a pleasant grip, soon rot and stretch when wet). The flat variety hold big favour as they seem to slide more easily through the hooks and D rings, while round laces appeal to some for exactly the opposite reasons. The round type seem to wear better and stretch less.

Most commonly, the quality forms are made from modern synthetic, anti-rot, materials, such as meraklon or polypropylene/nylon. These don't deteriorate as quickly and wear better than cotton varieties. Extra strength and reliability is gained from round, or tubular, laces which include a solid nylon core running the full inside length. Especially if the outer weave becomes snagged.

These days, laces rarely need to be long enough to reach and wrap around the back of the boot. Modern boot designs have done away with the need for such tactics. The loops of leather once found on the back of the boot cuffs have also generally disappeared, although some are still occasionally found, usually for cosmetic reasons.

HOOKS AND D-RINGS.

To avoid traditional lace holes, which would quickly let water through, metal D-rings (D shaped rings) are the definitive solution, keeping water entry to a minimum. (Anchored by studs. Occasionally with double studs through the same base plate. The rivet shaft seals its own hole as it's riveted. However, when used towards the top of the boot, as they need to be unthreaded for foot entry, they can be time consuming. For convenience, metal hooks allow laces to quickly wrap and fasten the top of the boots. (Some economy boots use only hooks)

Plastic versions (plasteel) adorn many fabric boots, but all versions deserve regular inspection for wear and tear. Cobblers and a lot of retail shops, provide a cheap service of replacing hooks and rings. (Some difficulties arise with boots that have waterproof linings).

Cheaper metal versions are prone to rust, but brass and special coatings can postpone or avoid such problems. Some hooks and D-rings are nickel plated, providing improved resistance to rusting and fatigue, while displaying a rather enhanced finish. Such details shouldn't influence a buying decision!

LININGS.

Boots can still be found with suede or leather linings but the majority now use modern synthetic versions. All primarily designed and used to wick away perspiration but also hard wearing, stable (3D construction), fast drying and anti-bacterial. (Keeping odours to a minimum).

The most common and popular of these is "Cambrelle ", (developed by I.C.I) which is used in differing thicknesses. (Cool Max may be another lining encountered). By effectively absorbing and wicking away foot moisture, the wearer's feet are kept cooler on the warmer days and by the same science, warmer in the cooler months.

Such linings, also being colour dye fast, often appear too soft to be durable, but the more common qualities provide loyal service for thousands of miles.

A common use of linings incorporates new ideas with tradition. A modern moisture absorbing material is used deeper in the forefoot area, while a suitable lining of leather lines the heel of the boot; usually only intended to keep the traditionalists happy.

The coverings of many midsoles also use similar materials (e.g, Ditex 75 to complement the finishing.

(Waterproof linings. See, Waterproof)

CUFFS.

Not for the first time, I have to mention that many styles and designs are available. The cuff is the area of the boot that encases the upper foot and ankle and provides it with support. Traditionally, boot cuffs were simple extensions of the leather boot, perhaps lined with some padding with a single support rib, or cuff of padding around the very top.

The problem with this simple design, although still suitable for many winter boots, is that while the leather (on leather boots) provides good support for the ankles against bending side-ways, it doesn't flex easily at the back when an ankle has to bend the foot down and forwards. This is why most boots utilise a ribbed design.

The patterns used vary, but usually ribbed cuffs (lined with a thin soft leather) appear as three soft padded bands or ribs running horizontally around the ankle of the boot. The idea is to provide the all-important support at the sides while easily flexing at the rear, as well as improving comfort and fit.

Of the better boots, the foam used to pad the cuff is often a P.U mixed with polyester foam, which has a longer life than most, while on cheaper versions occasionally the cuff's lining and outer are made from a P.V.C.

After a little use the cuff on boots will usually mould and shape to personalise a fit.

A few boots incorporating a little ski boot technology, (including the use of ski cables around the ankles) and includes one brand which uses external, articulated, plastic heels and cuffs, along with velcro strapping.

In recent times, a brand name, more traditionally associated with the sports trade, has introduced a fine range of walking footwear, with models featuring inflatable upper regions and cuffs, designed to improve the fit of a boot. There are obvious arguments for and against.

RESOLING.

Many people looking at modern soles, that don't use stitched welts, assume that they aren't resolable, but often these boots are more suitable for sole replacing than any other. Generally, only the decent quality boots merit a resoling once their rubber tread has worn thin, as the condition of the leather uppers will justify new soles. (Check the condition of the midsoles as well). Even if economy boots warrant a sole transplant, it might be cheaper to buy a completely new pair as replacement.

Boots

Many cobblers offer this service, or your local retailer may be able to recommend a specialist. Some manufacturers offer a resoling service (of their own boots) and chuck in new laces, footbeds and general clean up as well.

Unfortunately many owners of resoled boots carry with them reports of boots feeling a shade slimmer.

WATERPROOF?

Excluding boots that use a specific waterproof liner, boots can not be expected to be waterproof. "What!!?" I hear many walking persons exclaim! There are thousands of happy dry feet that use walking boots that are waterproof, but unfortunately, it's now impossible to guarantee, or categorically claim, that walking boots are waterproof.

I always say that a boot is only as waterproof as you proof it. Slapping a boot proofer on isn't good enough if you desire dry feet. With modern treatment, it's a case of building up many thin layers rather than one thick one, and of course, pay particular attention to any stitching.

Leather boots are a natural material, so it's impossible to assume that they will be watertight. Many people consider a boot that isn't waterproof, faulty. The boots shouldn't be assumed to be waterproof in the first place; this is the stance that most manufacturers now take.

Only boots that use an actual waterproof liner can be claimed as totally waterproof. (Even then there are many who would argue). Of the many waterproof liners available, Gore-tex is the most commonly used and recognized. (For full details. See Chapter 2 - Waterproofs) This firm accompany such boots with their own twelve month warranty against defects and failure of their lining. (Longer for waterproof clothing). The common denominator with all waterproof boot linings is that they should also be breathable. This is to avoid the damp conclusion your feet would suffer if just a waterproof but unbreathable bag was used. But note that this has nothing to do with improving the breathability of footwear. (When hard trekking the average foot perspiration over eight hours is around 200 grams!)

Modern waterproof boots, using waterproof linings, incorporate a

37

simple, easy to tape (make seams watertight) sock made from waterproof/breathable material. (Sometimes spot sealed). This is made independently from the boot and is then fitted and secured inside. (One patented process includes bonding the liner to the soles). This is a much better and more effective solution to boots originally made from waterproof fabrics. On modern waterproof fabric boots, it's not the fabric on the outside that keeps your feet dry, but the liner that does all the magic.

The sock itself is lined with a suitable material, protecting it against internal wear.

One use of Gore-tex in boots, is known as the "Gore-tex, Top dry" lining system. Found only on proof-tanned leather boots, the inner Gore-tex lining is then lined itself by a thin quality leather. This system is said to add protection from potential containments. (Inner contamination).

Anti-wicking tape fitted around the top inside edge of boots and their waterproof liners is a rare but excellent feature, helping reduce boot inners wicking moisture inside the boots. E.g, from contact with wet trouser hems.

Waterproof breathable liners also occasionally appear, in conjunction with leather boots. I'm not a fan, as I don't see the two as quite compatible. Waterproof linings are great for fabric boots, but the beauty of leather shouldn't need such an addition, particularly as you can only find this example on dearer boots. (They would be more interestingly used on relatively cheaper models). Quality boots featuring a waterproof lining also use quality leathers, which will last several years of use. A waterproof/breathable liner won't. Thus, you're landed with a pair of leather boots, which are still perfectly good for many more miles, but with a defunct liner that's given up the ghost. This can mean the overall breathability is impeded, plus, the possible disadvantage of water (e.g, over the top, from a stream) unable to escape.

WALKING SHOES. (A brief summary)

Essentially, true walking shoes and not just shoes that are practical,

Boots

should all feature the same general designs, styles and materials as boots. The only obvious difference is the absence of the higher cuff. (Some shoes are called three quarter height as they are not as low as a shoe, nor as high as a boot). You don't have to be so strict with larger sizing. Otherwise, apply all I've mentioned throughout these pages.

With many "walking shoes" that appear very similar to ordinary shoes but with flat, treaded soles and external tongues, I've always torn my hair out wondering why manufacturers insist upon adding decorative stitching patterns along the sides, as this makes them drastically less waterproof. I've heard rumours that they do exist without these fancy finishes, so if you want a shoe like this, my advice is to try and seek out a pair without the unnecessary decor.

CARE?

Leather; For extended service, boots need to be looked after. Leather is the most demanding and requires sympathetic treatment. Never force-dry leather boots. (i.e. next to a radiator, or even in a warm room). Water expands when it's heated, so if it can't evaporate quickly enough, it's likely to stretch, tear and damage the fibrous leather structure. Dry boots in a dry airy place. If wet inside, perhaps pack them with dry newspaper.

Proofings not only act as waterproof barriers but also condition the leather and keep it in tip top fitness. By the book (and this is one) you should reproof your boots after every outing you make in them. Dumping them at the back door, only to return hours later and bang the two soles together, shaking off the dried mud, isn't satisfactory. Leaving mud on them to dry can also over-dry the leather.

Under the tap or in a bucket, using a brush, (not wire), you should wash them down in cold water and then leave them to dry naturally.

When dry, apply the proofing of your choice. (Before this, if you think colouring is necessary, you can apply regular polish. Leave to dry before proofing). I couldn't possibly go into the highly strung world of what's the best proofing to use, but I will tell you not to let your boots see a bottle of linseed oil, cod liver oil, grease, even lard. (I've known cases of these being used, even one man who recommended Petroleum jelly!) Linseed oil is a classic leather treatment, but with many modern tanned leathers and plastic support liners, too much of it can ruin a pair of boots. Dubbin too, has been struck from the list, as it's now realized it rots stitching.

There are many good modern waxes available to choose from, but generally it's a good idea to stick with one once you've plumped for it. (Avoid waxes which are highly solvent based). Most should be rubbed well in with either rag or fingers, particularly at the stitching. (Take out the laces to get well into the grooves of the tongue and bellows). Leave for a little while and then wipe off surplus wax. (Again, wax shouldn't be dried by direct heat. For best results wax should be left to dry by curing). This leaves just a smooth layer of wax absorbed by the leather. Leave again to dry totally. Return and repeat the process two or three times.

Always proof boots with lots of thin layers rather than one thick one. The boots should be left with a smooth rubbery film finish, rather than a thick matting of wax. This only dries up and flakes off later. There are liquid versions of these waxes available but they are often misused. People rush for them convinced they are a more convenient alternative to the solid kind. Too much of these liquid waxes can be a bad thing, as they're more intended for occasional additional use, to reach deep into the leather. (In their liquid form they run the risk of over penetration). Their harsher content is suitable for revamping old boots that have over-dried and can overcome and chase out damaging solutions that accidently sometimes reach boots. (Using your walking boots while painting the outside of the house usually means you will spill paint or turpentine over them).

Recently, versions of the solid wax forms have appeared in a liquid state and are supplied with their own little brush. Dearer but with advantages that include being water based instead of solvent based they are instantly environmentally friendly. (+ Better for some glues used on soles). Not only quicker and easier, but the leather absorbs exactly as much as it needs, leaving any surplus on the surface waiting to be wiped away a short while later. Being able to apply it while the boots are still wet, is also a convenient improvement. Available for either leather or fabric boots. There is also an excellent wax cream spray.

Boots

Leather boots with Gore-tex, or similar, linings should be wiped clean with a damp cloth, dried as described and treated with normal shoe polish. Such a boot without waxes, etc, will breath easier than a conventionally proofed boot. (Quality polish will condition the leather. Or use water based waxes).

The one question many people ask is, "Do they need to be proofed before I use them?" Of course they do. It's just as feasible for it to rain on your first outing as on any other!

If your travels include peat bogs then your leather boots should be rinsed off with water as soon as you get the chance, as the rich acids found in such bogs can cause damage.

Fabric boots are a lot easier. Once you've cleaned away the surplus mud and grime, to help keep the suede in good nick, help the boots dry quicker and keep out light rain, spray the dry boots with one of the many spray products available displaying 'suitable for suede and fabric'. Usually silicone based, they don't try to increase the boots' waterproofness by simply blocking the holes of fabric and suede, interfering with the breathability, but coat them with a water-hating treatment, repelling water. There are many treatments that claim to virtually waterproof fabric boots, (including spraying inside) but this is dangerous territory. I've never known a completely successful application. All treatments for fabric boots, need regular top ups, as the proofings don't last long. Note that sprays available in aerosol form don't usually deliver or contain as much product as the smaller pump action spray bottles.

Only use mild soaps, if ever, making sure to rinse well afterwards, as strong detergents or softeners may destroy already adequate softening tanning oils. Stains may be removed with perchloroethylene.

Fabric boots which have a waterproof liner are already waterproof, so additional applications of sprays may be unnecessary, but can be a good idea, as breathable waterproof liners breath better when the exterior is dry. To help suede dry quicker and protect it from possible deterioration, occasional spraying with the before mentioned is required. In the winter months, wet fabric boots can also be colder.

With waterproof liners, be careful to avoid small sharp stones getting inside as these may puncture the waterproof barrier.

Some hooks and D rings can also require some looking after. To avoid rusting (oxidisation), some manufacturers have suggested smearing them with compounds such as petroleum jelly.

BOOT FIT. (Fit for the job?)

While the brand, style and price of a walking boot attracts much attention, actual concern for the right size, shape and fit seems much lower on the buyer's agenda. While the mountains of advice upon the heaps of different boot models available, still grow, the correct fitting is rarely referred to. This is surprising as it's the most important consideration. A pair of boots costing thirty pounds, that fit well, might be considered better than a a pair of boots at sixty pounds that don't.

Unfortunately, a common misconception for walkers, who have suffered from bruised toe nails, sore heels and aching toes, is to simply assume that their particular style and type of footwear was to blame. In fact, the vast majority of these cases are merely the result of ill-fitting boots; usually only due to incorrect sizing.

There are several rules and theories of how to achieve the correct boot fit. On finger down the back, or stand on one boot and lift heel of the other, are only two, but all are prone to error. Fingers down the back, but when the boots are laced or unlaced? How thick are your fingers? Are toes bent at the ends or should they be straight? Besides, all are unnecessary as it's really quite simple. Follow the three following measures and you can't go far wrong.

Assuming you would be wearing the socks you intend to wear with the boots, let us quickly cover the basics. First;

Toes: With all walking boots it's standard practice to go up a whole British size larger than your normal shoe size. Yes, a whole size larger! The first concern is not so much with the width and depth of the boot, but with it's length. (There are walkers who will protest that their boots are the same size as their shoes and cause no toe problems. I'm pleased for them, but there are always exceptions to every rule. There are some people who have got away with drink driving, but it's still not advisable.

Boots

If, once you've laced up the boots (not too tightly, but just comfortably firm), by pushing forward, while standing up, you can touch the end of the boot with one or more toes, then the boots are too small. Be very strict with this one rule, it's the most important.

Putting your foot inside footwear a whole size larger than you are used to, will feel "too big". This is to be expected, but the trick is to understand that what is the correct size for shoes is not the correct size for boots. The two main reasons we choose larger sizes, besides wearing extra and thicker socks, are...

A. Once out, walking for an hour or more, feet warm up and swell dramatically. Being on your feet all day at work or around the home, hasn't quite the same result. Although the classic cliche "buy boots late in the day" might help, it usually only adds to confusion.

B. More importantly, we should always leave plenty of room for our toes. It may only take five minutes of walking down the softest of hills to experience uncomfortable pressure on toes, but walking down something larger, with boots that are too short can be extremely painful. This will often lead to bruising or even loss of toe nails.

The same advice still applies to people interested in fabric boot designs as decent fabric boots still have the same hardened plastic toe caps.

Secondly...

The Heels: Everyone has a vague idea that sloppy heels in boots cause trouble. This is correct, "sloppy" being the operative description.

Heels and feet with thick socks in boots, a whole size larger, are rarely sloppy. It is wrong for people to think that a walking boot's heel should grip tightly. This can cause exactly the same symptoms. It's fairly obvious we should avoid sloppy heels and excess friction. Heels that have just a little movement, are in fact, fine. Thirdly, and finally...

The last of the three points to consider, is general comfort. If toes are clear, heels fine and bearing in mind that the boots are brand new, are they generally comfortable? Imagine how comfortable they will feel after softening and after five miles of walking. For example, if the boots feel firm around the feet now, then they'll feel positively tight, once out and about.

These points are only fundamentals for achieving the best fit. Plenty of other aspects could be considered; Extra slim women's models, extra wide boots, extra wide fittings, boots with different footbeds, or insoles, and boots available in half sizes, all add extra dimensions to the variations of successful fitting.

The three boot fitting guides simplified:

1. When laced up and standing, none of your toes should be able to touch the ends of the boots.

2. The heels shouldn't be sloppy or gripping. A little movement is ideal.

3. Considering the boots are brand new, they should feel generally comfortable. Remember, new shoes from a shoe shop feel firm at first.

In general:

Listen to your feet, not the number on the boot box. Ignore sizes written inside boots and let them serve only as a rough guide. One brand's size 43, or size 8.5, may feel smaller than a rivals 42 or size 8!

Remember, you're not buying ordinary shoes. Don't be afraid of a little extra room.

Don't let your usual instincts bully you into smaller boots.

If two different sizes feel the same, then go for the larger. There's no logic in going for the smaller size. When in doubt, always go for the larger size.

Always cater for your larger foot. Having one boot slightly too big rather than one slightly too small, is by far the lesser of the two evils. This is also why trying odd sized boots simultaneously, to gain a comparison test, can be misleading.

Slippage on heels can reduce once the boots and midsoles have softened up.

Boots

Try to do up the top hook, as this usually holds the heel in a boot.

Try not to confuse yourself by trying more than three or four different models on one occasion.

Don't turn up at the shop at twenty five past five!

CONTINENTAL AND BRITISH SIZINGS. (.5 = half size)

All manufacturer's sizings vary. This chart serves only as a rough guide.

Children's sizes.

26-------- 9	29--------11.5	32--------12.5	35--------2.5
27--------9.5	30--------12	33--------1.5	36--------3.5
28--------10.5	31--------12.5	34-------- 2	37-------- 4

Adult sizes

37-------- 4	40-------- 6	43--------8.5	46--------11
38-------- 5	41-------- 7	44--------9.5	47--------12
39--------5.5	42-------- 8	45--------10	48--------13

MANUFACTURERS. There is a staggering number of boot manufacturers, mostly good and now available. A smattering of the better names would include:

K-Shoes; This north of England manufacturer produces excellent and beautiful quality boots. (The Wainwright boot). Unusually high quality materials, manufacture, dreamy comfort and good value. Great to see excellent boots made in Britain as good, if not better, than boots from anywhere in the world.

Zamberlan and Scarpa; Both giants of the quality market, these Italian brands are forever popular. Note: Zamberlan also produce half sizes while Scarpa also produce extra wide fittings.

Karrimor's fabric K.S.B; A classic of fabric footwear. Top quality in every sense. For fabric footwear, these are particularly durable. Karrimor also have a quality range of leather K.S.Bs.

Line 7; A French brand of highly popular fabric footwear, mainly due to models with softness and attractive style.

Trezeta; Quality boots, doing a particularly good job of providing sound middle market value.

Daisy Roots (D.R); Produce fine value for money products, with a particularly popular line in waterproof fabric boots.

Brasher boots; Very popular and comfortable.

Hi-Tec; An endless choice of usually, fabric footwear. Comfortable, good value, stylish and popular. Boots for every budget.

Meindl; include some sound quality fabric boots, with a three hundred year history.

Reebok; A quality range with top of the range models offering unique extra features, while all provide comfort and style.

Koflach; Popular and quality plastic mountain boots.

Cima; Performance and value. Unusually good fit at this market.

Loveday (Loveson footwear); Good value for money.

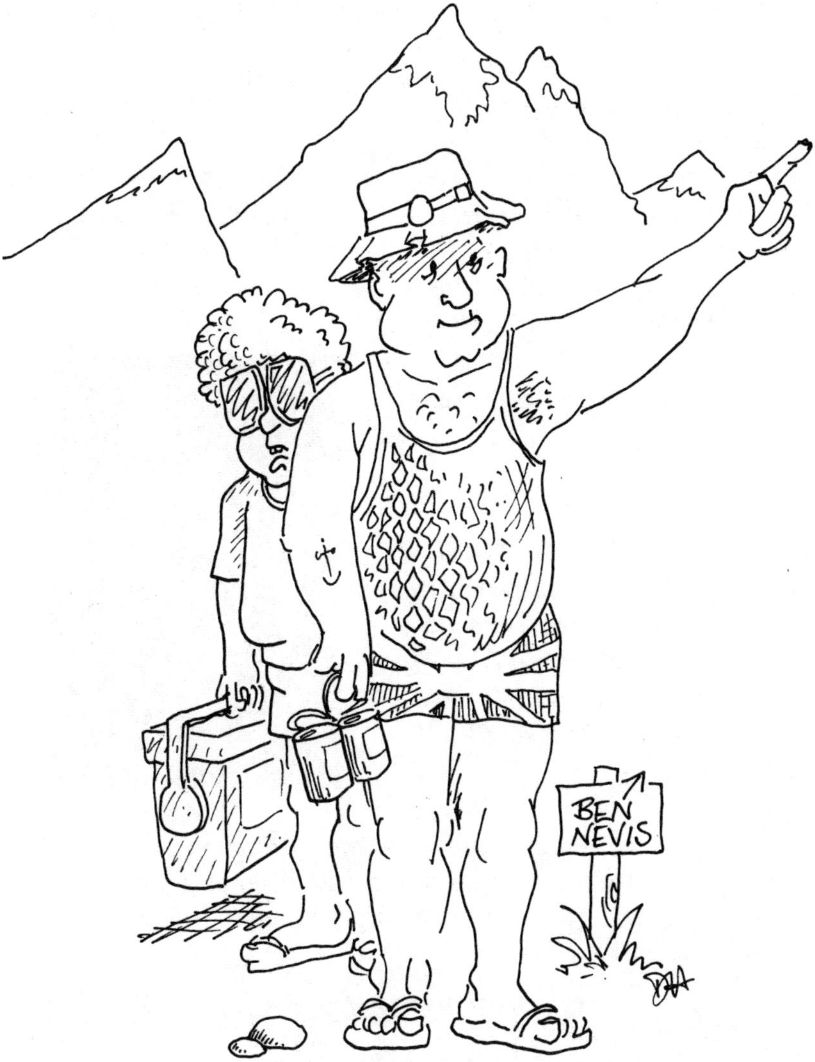
BEN
NEVIS

Quietly Superior

Since 1965 we've been manufacturing outdoor gear - gear that works.

Our Breakthru' system revolutionized waterproofs, we made breathables more breathable - after all that's what you pay for! Tough modern membranes and microfibres have made stiff, heavy waterproofs a thing of the past.

From Everest to Evesham, Breakthru' gives comfort and soft handle with toughness. A 1600 mile walk the length of the Canadian Rockies carrying a 75lb sack proved that, or a walk the length of Norway or 1000 mile trek across the Yukon or ....

Available from Specialist Retailers

Why not send for our brochure full of quietly superior gear that will give you quiet confidence in quiet garments.

CRAGHOPPERS

Batley, West Yorkshire
Tel: 0924 478481/443434. Fax: 0924 420014

WATERPROOFS.

For the British, one of the most important and perhaps most appreciated pieces of walking kit is the waterproofs. Not only, acting to keep us dry and comfortable and protecting us from harsher elements but, in some exposed areas of walking country, distancing us from the most hazardous of sometimes unforeseen weather extremes which can easily and quickly cause near fatal states of health. The possibility of exposure is vastly reduced by the protection of our portable and personal dry environment; our waterproofs.

Most of us can remember over recent years the rapid changes that have evolved and improved the nature of nearly all waterproofs today. (The first originally appeared around the 1870's as sea faring bleached canvas, prepared with linseed oils). Few may recall the original waxed cottons, or heavy neoprene and thick P.V.C garments of yesteryear but some still faithfully use their P.U coated nylon jackets that occurred during the early seventies. Remember the bright orange cagoules that adorned nearly every hill? Not only were the materials used basic but much of the garment's design had still a great way to go. There was a time when you would have to specify "waterproof" or "showerproof" garments, whereas today it's quite impossible to find a waterproof type, but only showerproof jackets for sale. Even boasting fully taped seams was a distinct bonus once upon a time.

Where the subject gets interesting is with the introduction of garments that are both waterproof and breathable. For the minority who might be unaware of the major disadvantages of all waterproofs up until the late seventies and of waterproofs that don't breathe today - the wearer soon becomes damp on the inside of the garment from their own internal humidity. Each and every one of us is constantly giving off a moisture vapour through our skin. If you put your hand inside a plastic bag, the inside will soon become damp due to the moisture vapour being unable to escape; this is exactly what happens when you wear an unbreathable waterproof garment. There are ways to help alleviate the problem - flapping fresh air inside for example- but none are satisfactory. The only consolation is that it was better to be damp and warm, than wet and cold! Far better! However for mountaineers this is dangerous, as damp clothing accelerates heat loss.

There was a time when no one expected a fabric that was waterproof and breathable to ever arrive. However, now each year at Trade Shows, manufacturers predict the time when unbreathable waterproof garments will be unavailable altogether.

Most outdoor shops now spend their waterproof energies promoting breathable garments, with non-breathables only really catering for the low budget customer. Needless to say there are as many price fluctuations as there are fabrics, but generally the performance of a breathable fabric can be vaguely scored by its price. (Note that it does pay dividends to wear suitable under garments. See Clothing chapter). Today, there are hundreds of different trade names for nearly as many different waterproof breathable materials (over 200 were once counted in a single Japanese outdoor magazine) and all offer differing degrees of performance, with a few claiming overall superiority. Whether this is because their products breathe more, are more resistant to flexing, perform better when wet, are able to stretch, or simply because they boast the highest waterproofing levels; all vary from one manufacture to the next. One thing however seems sure; all getting better and better.

Once the market was prominently dominated and arguably still is, by probably the most famous of all waterproof breathable materials - Gore-tex. Still a most impressive performer, the dominance seems, to some, to be declining since the on surge of dozens of other alternatives. The most memorable taste left by rival blurbs, is the highlighting of equal performance at lower cost. Gore (makers of Gore-tex fabric) always provide a strong case for favouring their products, with back-up service being one of their highest advantages. But for us sea of mortal users seeking to find the best waterproof breathable fabric available, our quest is now nigh-on impossible. "Who to believe" has long since eclipsed the "look into their eyes" stage. A few years ago, I might have been brave enough to try to tell you which was the best, but not now. I'm not stupid enough, or perhaps clever enough, to attempt such a task. I have in fact seen many precise, scientific measurements, tests, graphs, charts and figures all designed to prove that a given fabric performs well, or better. However, due to the sheer quantity of similar claims now available, I can safely draw only one conclusion; it doesn't really matter too much whose fabric you choose. Many seem much of a muchness, or are too close to call.

Are comparisons worth making? Should it be our concern? After all, measuring just how breathable a garment is, in real terms, has always been a ridiculous aspiration. Variations that provide different results from the same jacket and provide fluctuating facts for differing manufacturers, all go to make the entire subject rather futile. For example, what a user has had to eat, their sex, the humidity of the atmosphere, the temperature differentiation between the outside and the inside of the garment; all these are crucial variables. Failing that, does 3.5 litres of moisture vapour transmission, through a square metre of fabric, over twenty four hours, mean that much to you? Many of the cheaper low budget breathables, while legally claiming good breathability, in actual usage terms offer hardly any improvements over traditional garments. Instead of becoming damp after ten minutes, perhaps it's now fifteen? It's the pricing and pole position in the shop ranges that can give an indication of their standard and to a garments breathing capabilities. A simple jacket intended for rambling may be considerably cheaper than a jacket designed to perform on top of Everest, along with extra features, but made from exactly the same material.

Quality waterproof breathables are relatively expensive but these qualities shouldn't be confused with durability or life expectancy. Coincidentally they will usually outlive a cheaper traditional waterproof but the initial extra cost incurred refers to the performance and comfort they provide while the garment lasts and is not related to how long it will last. In a way, you're not paying for the product, but for the improved comfort it will offer over the same period of time.

Generally, all waterproof fabrics split into either of two fields:

A. There are sprays; The most common example is a taffeta nylon sprayed, coated, and waterproofed on the inner side with P.U. (Polyurethane). There are many different qualities, the better, providing three or four applications, building up a more durable finish. Sprayed fabrics are cheap, effective, but eventual poorer resistance to flexing and internal abrasion make their durability lower than ...

B. Laminates; a waterproof membrane, which is then usually laminated to other traditional fabrics for added strength and are more tolerant to flexing, (British standards require faultless performance with the minimum of 9000 flexes. One of the best laminates can withstand up to 100 times this). But laminates are relatively dear. They can eventually delaminate.

(As dry breathable waterproofs breathe better than waterlogged ones, it has been stated that laminates waterlog quicker than coated fabrics).

Both sprayed and laminated methods can produce waterproof and breathable fabrics.

There are now two main methods of creating waterproof breathables using spray technology or laminates:

The original; Poromeric, or microporous = using holes providing a sieve system. A simple logic to understand; holes too small for water molecules to get in (waterproof) but large enough for moisture vapour molecules to escape (breathable). See - Goretex, section to follow.

The second; Non-poromeric (without holes), or hydrophilic systems, use molecular chains; one water loving (hydrophilic) and one water hating (hydrophobic). Evaporated perspiration divides into separate molecules. (When they reform, they recreate condensation). These are attracted by the fabric's hydrophilic molecules but in conjunction with the pushing motion of the fabrics water hating molecules, the evaporated perspiration molecules are wicked or transported away, accelerated by the user's garment's higher internal humidity, rather like stepping stones, through and out to the other side of the material.

(Another option includes waterproofs that enlist the use of wash-in "waterproofings" that you buy off the shelf. Hmmmm...?)

The name Gore-tex, for many, has almost become a generic description of breathable waterproof fabric. No doubt about it, it certainly did lead the way, beginning with the problem of initially having to explain to the public that there was a problem in the first place. In this respect, as the father of its field, its fitting that its physics, designs and features are explored, as most of the details concerned can easily be applied to most other waterproofs.

Waterproofs

GORE-TEX.

What eventually changed for ever the whole unhappy situation of uncomfortable clamminess on the inside of waterproofs and influenced other attitudes across the entire industry was the advent of Gore-tex. Arriving on our shores in 1977, for the first time walkers could wear a waterproof garment without the fear of becoming damp and clammy on the inside. The well documented science of how the product actually works revolves around a kind of sieve system. A membrane, made from expanded polytetraflouroethylene (or rather P.T.F.E, for short! Made from flourine & carbon atoms) contains billions of tiny holes, (.000008 of an inch) conveniently smaller than water molecules (rain) but large enough to allow moisture vapour molecules (your moisture vapour) through and out. For those of you who might not have already encountered the now almost legendary magic figures, here they are! There are nine billion pores to every square inch of membrane, which are twenty thousand times smaller than a water molecule but seven hundred times larger than moisture vapour molecule. Every walking and camping shop sales assistant should be able to mutter these digits in their sleep!

The moisture vapour is forced out through the membrane by the higher internal temperature of the garment. This is why, as with all good breathable waterproofs, it is no longer necessary (in fact it's counterproductive) to choose garments too large, as this reduces the effectiveness of their breathability. Extra room inside a jacket means the difference in external and internal temperatures (pressure) is reduced, along with breathable performance. Simply go for sensible standard sizing, ensuring that you are able to wear a thick jumper, or fleece, underneath. Note that breathable waterproofs suffer limited success in humid climates.

Although relatively tough, the thin membrane wouldn't be strong enough to make up waterproof garments on its own, so it's strengthened and protected by laminating (bonding) it to other traditional fabrics. If the membrane is sandwiched in-between two other fabrics, it becomes a three layer Gore-tex fabric. (A composite with the outer and inner/backing fabric). Laminated to just the one, and it's a two layer. For years the three layer version was the only standard method of using the membrane. Many outer protective materials were tried and experienced, including polycotton, (but that absorbed too much moisture), 1000 denier nylons, (but they became too stiff and provided less protection against contamination), and standard taffetas, (but they eventually were found to be prone to delaminating). These are just a few examples.

From the dozens of Gore-tex fabrics available today, taslan (a mid weight nylon), polyester mixes or fine micro nylons are utilised on contemporary garments. Each fabric offers its own characteristics and is selected by various clothing manufacturers to complement and provide suitable performances for differing types of garments. For example, a soft and supple polyester suits a leisure style, whereas the more abrasion resistant ruggedness required for a pure outdoor hill walker's jacket, means that a taslan fabric is more appropriate. The main advantage a three layer fabric has over it's two layer cousin, is its durability but, while its presence is still large and is still favoured by many, its sales percentage seems now to be giving way to the lighter, more flexible and, most importantly, more breathable, two layer products.

On the three layer Gore-tex fabrics, the third layer of fabric, used for the inside of garments, is a lightweight mesh type of the knitted scrim. (Tricot knit). This is to protect the inside of the membrane from internal abrasion, eliminate any cold feeling against bare skin and, if necessary, absorb a small amount of moisture. This serves to store it if the fabric is unable to dissipate an excess amount of vapour quickly enough. On two layer versions, (also used for insulated garments), where the inner scrim isn't used, usually a simple drop nylon liner, or more recently, loose mesh, helps protect it from the inside and improve the garments general comfort. (Mesh also breathes more easily). Some thoughtful manufacturers use a combination of mesh body linings and smooth nylon linings only for the arms, as mesh can cling when sliding on and off.

It has now been found that anti-wicking lining materials are a wiser choice because if a small area (e.g, small of the back) does become damp through excessive perspiration, then the problem would be magnified as a high wicking fabric quickly spreads it across the entire area. Combated mainly by the addition of anti-wick trims around the inside hem of jackets

Waterproofs

but still a potential problem with wicking liners is that they can also cause a rising damp effect when in contact with wet trousers.

Common for a while, but with the improvement in the durability, of the two layer fabrics, Gore-tex light is a third alternative method of membrane use. It's popularity seems to have declined recently in Britain but still remains a good consideration for more pure leisure orientated products. The membrane is bonded directly only to the garment's liner, independent of the garment's outer fabric. This has the advantage of placing the breathable membrane close to the wearer's skin, achieving the maximum location for moisture vapour transmission.

Gore-tex Z-liners were also a one time common and popular method of construction. Here the membrane is left (laminated only to a thin mesh for strength) to hang independently inside and in between the loose outer and lining of a normal garment. (Sometimes used for cycling/golfing jackets in it's own right). This system provides a very flexible finish, but not as tough as traditionally laminated fabrics. The main advantage with drop liners is the avoidance of taping all the garments external seams, not only reducing the bulk of stiff seams but also leaving the designers free to create more complex and detailed external designs; particularly favoured by ski clothing manufacturers. It's cheaper too! One argument in their favour is that because the liner is shielded by the outer materials, it's also protected from the chilling affects of cold wind and rain which may encourage condensation to occur.

(Stretch Gore-tex is available for use in socks. The G.T.X membrane is laminated to a stretched lycra fabric. When the lycra retracts you can then restretch it, giving the appearance of a fully stretchable membrane).

Confusion often arises when wearers are aware that the outside of their three, or two, layer Gore-tex products become saturated from the rain. Thought by some to be signs of leaking this is simply referred to as "wetting out". What happens is that while the membrane itself remains waterproof, the materials selected for use on the outside of the fabric do not. This doesn't actually cause the user a real problem, but dry garments breath better than wet ones, so the occasional application of a suitable spray (available from outdoor shops) will reduce the problem and help repel, and shed water. New garments already come with this treatment, (Hydrophobic = water hating) but in time, it wears off. However, occasionally a light warm tumble dry or warm ironing can revitalize this protection, which at its best, resembles water rolling off a duck's back. D.W.R, and fluorochemical, or fluorocarbon, coatings are just two descriptions of this overlooked element of general performance.

No longer a regular problem with modern waterproofs, but a waterproof jacket made from waterproof material is only as a waterproof as its seams. Unfortunately, while a jacket may be made from perfectly waterproof fabric, the holes at every seam, left behind by the sewing needle, will allow easy penetration by any reasonable force of rain. Once upon a time seams were simply rolled and doped, (stitch holes plugged with glue) but Gore (producers of Gore-tex fabric) influenced the introduction and encouraged the practice of fully taping seams. In their own particular case a new type of tape had to be developed (Gore-seam tape) as the inner scrim on a three layer fabric meant that adhesive tape couldn't make an adequate watertight connection with the membrane hidden below. Their own tape though is applied with heat (600C) and enables a slight melting of the tape to forge through and past the mesh scrim. (Sealed at 50lbs an inch).

Some manufacturers have now improved and reduced the thickness of each garment seam so that more contact between the tape and fabric can be made, improving even further the watertight barrier. A form of doping still exists with some products, where at crossroad seams, a solution is applied over the seam's thread, which then blocks the possible progression of any water that might be wicked along it's path and on into other joins. (Unusual and rare, but some use a special non-wicking Teflon treated thread). A while ago, even Gore-tex garments could be found with only the main seams taped. Today strict quality regulations enforce that all internal seams are dealt with accordingly, sustaining a garments waterproof warranties from the fabric manufacturers, but a watertight guarantee from the clothing manufacturer too.

The introduction of the membrane initially incurred a few teething problems, which included contamination from regular dirt and human oils, which in turn broke its surface tension and allowed external water easily to pass through. But that "phase one" Gore-tex has long since been superseded by a second version, specially coated with oil-hating substances and therefore impervious to alien bodies, but less breathable,

Waterproofs

which we now find in all Gore-tex waterproofs. Phase one Gore-tex is still used in certain applications, such as tents (not all Gore-tex tents), Bivi bags and clothes that don't claim to be waterproof. Particularly present in Bivi bags, its use by some is preferred as oxygen is easily passed through and users don't end up suffocating on carbon monoxide. But of course these products do have to be kept spotlessly clean to maintain their waterproof protection. Seafarers, or just visitors to the beach, might find that their G.T.X (Gore-tex) performance is impaired once it's been exposed to salt water. This is easily remedied by rinsing out any sea water, with cold fresh water, from the inside of the garment.

Does it really work? The basic answer is yes, although I have encountered many dissatisfied users. However, compared to the millions of happy devotees, this small minority, has either a genuine cause for complaint, or falls into the category of the misinformed. Of all the different products available throughout the world, I doubt that few rival the lack of understanding associated with breathable waterproof products. Who's fault all that is, is open debate, but the damage has now been done, so let's make the best of a bad lot.

"This waterproof/breathable jacket you sold me. It doesn't work. I'm sweating!".

Basically, breathable waterproofs DO NOT STOP YOU SWEATING. Perspiring is a bodily function designed to cool your body's core temperature. If the climate is too hot, or you've performed a heavy activity and increased your metabolism then your body is likely to find the increase in heat uncomfortable. Water is then released on the surface of our skin (perspiration), which evaporates and draws off heat, thus helping to cool us down. (In one hour you can lose up to two pints of water during heavy activity). This has nothing to do with breathable waterproof fabrics. How can a fabric stop you perspiring? It can't! Non-breathables trap moisture vapour, making you damp. Breathables don't. That's the only difference.

Occasionally you are still likely to find yourself becoming damp and uncomfortable on the inside of a good breathable waterproof garment, but this is usually because you are producing vapour faster than the fabric can dissipate it, or faster than the earth's atmosphere can absorb it. The crucial difference between breathables and non-breathables is that in certain conditions it might be necessary to keep your waterproof on, because it's still raining for example, or perhaps because the wind would chill you too quickly due to your now damp clothing. (Any fabric that's waterproof, can also be deemed windproof). If you were forced to continue with a non-breathable, it would only increase the problem, whereas a breathable waterproof would enable its user at least to enjoy its wind-proof protection in the knowledge that once the user eventually came to rest and reduced his rate of exertion, the fabric will still continue to dissipate the internal moisture, enabling its owner to dry out whilst still wearing the protective shell.

(It's important for the waterproof/breathable's potential performance to wear the right undergarments. E.g, no cotton. See Clothing chapter).

For a waterproof fabric to be able to claim that it is waterproof, in Britain, means it's able to withstand a hydrostatic head (or water entry pressure) of 200cm. A hydrostatic head is the measured height at which a single column of continuous water was dropped onto the fabric, before it began to show signs of leaking. Gore-tex boast a measurement of over 4000cms, but many quality waterproofs achieve similar impressively high standards. The height that the column of water reaches simulates the pressure or severity of different rain types, but you might wonder if any ever reach such pressures as 4000cms? The main advantage high H.H measurements serve, other than just rain protection, is when you kneel down in waterproof trousers on wet ground for example. The pressure on

Waterproofs

the fabric, at the knee, quickly becomes much greater.

Each page in this book could be filled with an illustration of a particular style and design of waterproof jacket and trousers. Over the years, like cars, their designs have become similar and more familiar, with good ideas staying the course, forever being refined, and bad ideas, or just simply unpopular ones, weeded out, only to live on in discontinued classic or near antique products that are occasionally spotted roaming the hills.

Different manufacturers, all using similar fabrics, now need to woo their customers by the skill in which they incorporate all the little design features that go to finalise a good usable product. Designing a hood correctly, can make a difference (breathable fabrics with a small peak, to aid breathing), not using velcro strips with fabric that would attract it, are only two of the many considerations for designers. The classic area for a design to vary lies around the pockets. This is an awkward subject with many dissatisfied users who have found soaking wet tissues in their pockets. There have been terrible pockets in the past, but it seems that most designers are now wising up to, or are now taking the effort to avoid what causes pocket leakage. Unfortunately, no pocket can confidently be deemed waterproof. To be fair it's virtually impossible to waterproof a pocket where there's always going to be an opening. (Like the neck, collar and cuffs of a jacket). Where most manufacturers have come impressively close, virtually achieving a waterproof pocket, is at the chest. Not present on most of the standard starter waterproofs, but very common on the quality breathables, are chest pockets, or map pockets. Accessed horizontally, from inside the front storm flap, next to the main zip, these ingenious designs are the safest and usually most spacious of pockets. (There's no need to undo the front zip. Handy in wet conditions). Problems with pocket designs, including the choice of materials, have included the wearer's vaporised moisture pumping directly into a pocket.

Only in recent times has one of the classic problems seemingly been overcome and even then only because the actual cause was discovered. Even with thick broad protective flaps covering the main front zip of a jacket, many designs seemed plagued by water seepage, which managed to find its way through the front zip and inside the garment. A relatively recent discovery, was that the thread used to stitch together such clothing was also wicking and transporting moisture directly along its path and onto the strip of knitted material to which zips are attached. This then allowed easy access inside the garment. Good modern designs now avoid this problem, by eliminating the seams from making contact with any part of the zip. A second minor offending cause was found to be protective storm flaps which backed by wicking materials. (On Goretex garments, the same knitted weave as on the inside of the body fabric). These materials were contributing to the same results. Again, good modern designs now use non-wicking materials to line such areas, unless a double, fold over, storm flap is used. (Two flaps, one folding over the other).

FEATURES.

Although hundreds of different designs utilising dozens of features, or even variations of features, continuously create a list too long to ever hope to cover, the following are most of the standard, good, and classic features to look out for. Different products, designed for different jobs, commonly incorporate different features. Choosing a design, you will be able to decide which features are necessary, which you think you are likely to appreciate and which you think are unnecessary, not only to avoid unnecessary expense, but also to keep weight and pack size to a minimum.

Zips. All jackets, at the main body zip, use double ended (or two way) types. This is where a second zip puller can also be operated from the bottom end. Handy if extra leg room is needed; when sitting in the car, climbing over a stile, cycling, or reaching for trouser pockets. Some people have difficulty doing these zips up at first, usually simply because they haven't initially pulled both pullers right down to the very bottom of its length. The knack is quickly acquired, but doing them up without looking can sometimes help. (Over the head smock garments are now very rare and unsuitable for walking, as difficulties with controlling the wearer's temperature arise). Some high quality breathables on the inside may also utilize a lighter pair of zips, spaced internally on either side of the main entry zip. These are to accommodate the addition of a zip-in fleece. (See Clothing chapter).

At the very top of most main entry zips, a small piece of fabric is included. This important feature sits flat against the inside of the zip, protecting your chin from the discomforts of a cold zip, and also helping to avoid painful encounters for bearded users.

Waterproofs

On real walking jackets, intended for any standard of country walking, it is imperative that the front zip should be protected by an external storm flap. (A flap of waterproof material that covers the main zip). Even if you find touch and fasten (velcro) closures annoying, it has been found that these fastening systems provide better anti-water finishings than studded versions. Studs, which are more at home on general leisure garments, may be considered if a second flap is used under the first. With velcro storm flap closures, the better products will also incorporate two small studs, at the top and bottom, as these areas can become haggard and require positive closures to maintain the highest protection. (One thoughtful velcro flap closure leaves a break midway along it's length. This greatly aids opening).

HOODS Many variations of hood design now exist, but all usually lean towards a given use or activity. Walking cags will usually feature a full hood, while more general leisure styles may enlist a simple roll away, into the collar, design. The more protective styles now nearly always incorporate the excellent addition of a wired visor. This is a small peak around the top and sides of the hood, that also conceals a malleable wire. This can then be moulded and shaped at will to whichever angle is convenient. This design vastly increases your comfort and visibility in rainy conditions. Many manufacturers now prefer to tailor away the side pieces, as this can impede sideways vision. As mentioned earlier, the better peaks will be trimmed with anti-wicking materials. To complement the visor or peaked designs, hood or face draw cords are added, enabling a snug fit around the face to be appreciated, particularly important in heavy windy wet weathers. (Particularly if you're a spectacles wearer). The draw cords require no fiddly knots, as they all feature fast self locking, or spring lock, cord grips, which are not only important with wet cold hands or when wearing gloves, but simply make life a lot easier.

Increasingly more common on some of the most modest of jackets, hood volume adjusters are also a convenient feature. Many different methods exist, but the general design is usually a simple draw cord and gripping toggle at the rear of the hood, which can be adjusted to either increase, or decrease, the hood's size. This improvement in fit can instantly improve the wearer's vision, and permits adjustment according to differing severities of weather.

Not so common and only usually found on the more adventurous mountaineering jackets, neck draw cords will also improve protection in extreme conditions. Making snug the garment's collar around the neck, they reduce the possibility of the elements getting in, but also reduce convection. (Warmth being directly pumped out through the top to the jacket). Often an elastic stretch cord may be used and occasionally also feature lock-together toggles at the front of the neck, to complete the full snugness and circumference around the neck.

Roll away hoods come in nearly as many different designs and finishings details as jackets, but all should include at least a draw cord around the face. Some feature a soft peak to aid eye protection, but only rarely will you find a roll away hood which also features a small wired visor.

Once, straight cut designs were the norm (still with starter jackets), but now most embody waist draw cords, as well as the more usual hem cords. Waist draw cords not only improve the fit of garments, reducing wind flap, but help to keep warmth in and cold out. (Remembering how breathables work, they can also improve their breathability). Without the use of various draw cords which create separate chambers, a jacket can easily resemble a bellows pump. With your movement inside, warm air can be pumped out quickly with jackets also suffering from convection.

Most waist draw cords are referred to as external, as the accessible parts of the cord protrude externally out through the front of the garment. Internal draw cords (cord ends hanging loose inside the garment) aren't as typical and feature more usually on general purpose leisure clothing. Internal cords aren't as suitable for walking jackets as it would be impractical to have to open up the entire jacket, exposing yourself and your inner clothing to the elements each time you wished to adjust the settings. Draw cords should be made from nylon or polypropylene as, unlike cotton, they won't rot or stiffen in cold conditions. (Occasionally elastic is used).

Recently, many manufacturers have ingeniously begun to do away with the, sometimes annoying, surplus loose flapping ends of draw cords by cleverly hiding them and their toggles inside external pockets. However, this is usually only an improved finishing feature for leisure garments as this design can also sometimes be inconvenient out in the field during harsh weather.

Waterproofs

JACKETS, which incorporate tougher materials specifically for high-wear areas, (e.g, shoulders & elbows) are becoming less common, as it's generally been realised that what was previously thought to be among the weaker materials is tough enough for nearly all jobs. The breathable membrane or spray will usually conk out way before the surface material would. Traditionally these designs only really appealed to the consumers "wise buy" conscience, conjuring up thoughts of such jackets being harder wearing and lasting longer. Now the demand dictates lightness and therefore heavy weight shoulder patches are limited. The only occasions when reinforced segments of a jacket (and trousers) are genuinely necessary arise for use in climbing or mountaineering products. Only here, where excessive use, of ropes, place the garments wear and tear life expectancy lower than the membrane or spray's, is the inclusion of tougher fabrics justified.

CUFFS. You can still find examples of differing cuff designs, usually on the cheaper products, but for some years, one design has been prominent. The simple velcro wrap around (external velcro adjustable) cuff will be found on nearly all waterproofs today. A single piece of protruding fabric, armed with a piece of velcro, spurring from the arm's single seam, simply and effectively raps around the wrist and fastens down against a strip of velcro that also rests, externally, around the cuff. This design's advantages far outweigh its few disadvantages. Complaints that, unlike the traditional elasticated cuffs that lived inside a straight external sleeve, hands get wet as they are unprotected, are counterbalanced by this design being more waterproof. As it only contacts the main arm seam, there is no additional taping required. The strip of velcro (or touch and fasten fabric) that's stitched to the outside of the cuff, is easily and effectively taped with single strips directly to the reverse side. Other advantages include the choice of fastening tight the cuff around the outside of glove cuffs (when walking) or on the inside of glove cuffs (if climbing). This simple design can also be easily operated with cold or gloved hands.

Recently a clever improvement has begun to materialise in the form of self tightening cuffs. A feature present on some gloves for years. This design is still limited in appeal as it's relatively expensive and will usually only be found on the dearer mountaineering jackets.

PIT ZIPS. Again, increasingly more common, the addition of underarm zips to aid ventilation, when necessary, have proved a popular and comfort improving feature, particularly with many walkers who find over-heating a regular problem.

The cut and design of arms, while not usually a specific feature, can usually justify some attention. Arms should avoid seams over the very top of shoulders which might falter under contact with the heaviest area of rucksack abrasion. Some jackets feature "bear hug" elbows, a tailoring of the arm, using tucks, which comfortably follows the elbow's natural contours. Underarm gussets allow improved overhead reach, reducing the effects of arm sleeves shooting up the wrist.

OVER TROUSERS. Sometimes known as waterproof leggings, waterproof over-trousers don't boast as many differing features, although all manufacturers use slightly different cuts, including such details as "diamond crutches". Usually elasticated at the waist, some users may prefer designs that also incorporate drawstrings to tie and tighten.

On the more deluxe models, knee length zips are now a regular feature, which enables easy access to boots. The zips travel up the outside of the trouser and finish at the knee, but the most important detail to note is whether the zip is backed by a full bellows, as one without will easily allow water through. Maybe a minor disadvantage only for shorter people, but bear in mind that with the addition of such zips, the overall trouser length can't be shortened. Some thoughtful manufacturers, only start the zip from around two inches above the hem, which provides some room for alteration.

Much dearer and only truly necessary if you are wearing crampons are full length zipped trousers. With zips that travel the full length of the side of each trouser leg and up onto the waist, these designs eliminate the need to slide the trousers on, instead wrapping around and fastening up. Trying to work out what goes where, when it's blowing a gale, can resemble some kind of mensa test. It is impossible to protect zips against water leakage from the inside, so all use external protective flaps over the outside of zips, usually fastened by studs. For winter walkers wearing fleece or other warm under trousers, these studs can provide an effective air conditioning system when the zips are left undone with only the studs in place.

Waterproofs

(Note: Descriptions. Shell = a waterproof/windproof garment, with inner seam tape exposed. Jacket = with a liner. Although both could be described as a shell, due to the equal protection).

MANUFACTURERS; the following are only a selection of some waterproof manufacturers of note.

Craghopper; A top quality British manufacturer producing a forever popular and successful range, easily remaining one of the best labels in waterproofs. Manufacturers since 1965, their starter "CAG JAC" models, are almost used as a generic description for all P.U nylons. Specialising in top quality highly breathable garments, Craghopper boast an unusual level of instant comfort as great bastions of drop liner systems and beautifully lightweight micro fibres. They produce many styles, including mountaineering and hillwalking, but also feature unusually well fitting ladies garments.

Berghaus; This label is synonymous with quality outdoor equipment. Being the first in Britain to use Gore-tex, they have constantly maintained their position as one of the handful of leading waterproof manufacturers. (Many of their designs set the standards of others). Their status and reputation are rarely surpassed. Excel in mountaineering protection.

Sprayway; From their relatively humble beginnings and first tinkerings with Gore-tex, Sprayway have grown into a beautiful swan. A company with their finger on the pulse, these mainstream Manchester manufacturers shine when producing good looking (and functional) garments at relatively sensible prices. They regularly annually achieve the highest sales of any one particular Gore-tex garment in the country. First class.

Mountain Equipment; The resurgence of this historic and once gigantic of names, means M.E are back. Top quality north west manufacturers, they know their business and excel in designs associated with the more extreme climates and conditions. (But also cater for hillwalking and travelling. Also strong in insulated extreme winter waterproofs).

Phoenix; A sound manufacturer they certainly know how to make waterproof clothing. Far north of England based, their standards are of the highest quality.

Karrimor; This British and traditional rucksack manufacturer has finally and genuinely broken into the clothing market. This giant of outdoor equipment names produce many excellent garments. These are world class products and appeal to a large range of markets.

Lowe Alpine; Using a particularly high grade of waterproof/breathable material these are excellent quality garments. The claims are impressive and offer great value. Now a distant relative of it's original "Latok" former self, Lowe clothing still regularly maintains it's American/Canadian look.

RUCKSACKS

A bugbear of some forms of camping is the requirement to take every step accompanied by the weight of your camping equipment and wardrobe. A rucksack, packed with tent, stove and sleeping bag, transforms the walker and camper into a backpacker; often seen as a higher form of admirer of the wild and wonderful places. The backpacker can go where the wind blows him and feel at peace with his knowledge of being totally self sufficient.

Call them what you will, a knapsack or packersack usually refer to smaller day sizes, while backpacks and rucksacks relate to the larger versions needed for excursions of a few days or more.

Various forms of packs carried on the back, have a history nearly as long as man, but the first most notable era of bags, designed specifically for the leisure user, is the external framed age. Inspired by some early American Red Indian designs, mass produced external framed sacks first appeared by the nineteen thirties using tubular steel. Soon aluminium would supersede steel in lightweight popularity but offer a significant reduction in strength. By the late nineteen seventies lightweight and rustproof plastic frames were in use. Anyone that ever visited a camping site in the seventies (or any American national park today) can not fail to have witnessed one of these designs, which totally dominated all rucksack manufacturers' way of thinking.

Different shapes and sizes evolved for slightly different purposes, but basically a square frame was strapped to the user's back, from which a soft sack, or bag, was suspended. As well as having better air circulation around the user's back (still unmatched by modern bags) the idea was to spread the load over a larger area of your body's frame, while keeping the bag's contents spread and distributed evenly. This helped maintain a safe stable carry with a better line of gravity than a tear drop shape of sack hanging low on you back. For this they were effective, but all suffered one general criticism. The user could never become quite comfortable as the rigid frame, strapped to his shoulders

Rucksacks

and waist, would act rather like a splint, inhibiting movement.

In 1973, a Newcastle company known as Berghaus, began manufacturing and introduced to Europe the first internally framed rucksacks. Simplified frames situated inside the pack (anatomically pre-shaped) would offer more internal space, a better carry as the mass weight is much closer to the user's back and, made from the right materials, eliminate the old problem of rigid restriction. Frames made from malleable alloy (often aircraft aluminium, HE 30TF) and formed in flat, ruler type, lengths (sometimes referred to as internal staves) could flex, even mould, to personalise a fit, while maintaining the all-important strength for load distribution. This is how virtually all rucksacks in Britain appear today.

By ensuring the correct size and fitting, it can be said that modern sacks aren't carried, but worn.

(Traditionalists may refer to external framed bags as backpacks while internal frames are larger rucksacks).

LOAD BEARING

The most important criterion a rucksack has to achieve is good load bearing. The human frame is not ideally suited to carrying heavy loads. Early back packs would soon highlight this by inducing aching shoulders and backs. But it has been recognised that the hips (not waist) are strong and apt at transferring weight down through the legs. Particularly strong pelvis regions occur around the rear centre, near the base of the spine, (iliac crest) and provide all modern bags with the main target for most weight distribution. This area is known as the lumbar region.

With this in mind, all modern bags have hip belts. This thick belt that fastens around your lower waist, resting on your hips, is designed to take the majority of the sack's weight, while the shoulder straps serve more in keeping the bag upright and stable.

The use of a good hip belt helps achieve a good line of gravity. You should not have to lean too far forward when carrying a sack. A good line of gravity means you are able to stand vertically, avoiding having to slouch. The higher the weight the better. Looking at the profile of a sack-laden walker, an imaginary line can be drawn down through the bulk of the sack, across to the body of the user (above the hips. Smoothly travelling into them) and down through the legs. A good line has a mild curving and sweeping course, while a bad example would have a greater bend and more pronounced shift in direction towards the carrier's body.

(A climber would prefer a lower centre of gravity to avoid becoming top heavy when climbing at angles).

A well packed rucksack will have heavier items at the top and be able to stand upright by itself.

BACK SYSTEMS.

Unlike Grandfather's rucksack, modern back designs are all anatomically shaped with the main improvement being the addition of a comfortable hip belt, along with many other finer details. By the mid-eighties the main buzz word in rucksack design was "adjustable". Recognising that the best load-carry relates to achieving the best fit, meant that a barrage of adjustable back systems would eventually engulf the market. The many different types run into dozens but all follow the same basic principles. Different sizes of people, producing different back lengths, mean that a sack with full adjustability of it's own back length can provide the user with the ultimate in personal, tailor made, fitting. The fit of a rucksack is everything. (See; The right fit of a rucksack)

The majority of such bags feature shoulder straps that can travel higher or lower, lengthening or reducing it's own back length, while much rarer are back systems where the hip belt journeys up or down. The disadvantage with the latter is a poor line of gravity for shorter people, as the bottom of the sack can hang over and below their pelvic level. The generally better alternative of the moving shoulder strap systems, avoid this, but even then, if catering for shorter people, could become top heavy, as the load is left towering above the user's head.

These systems also usually require parallel frames (two vertical bars) rather than the much more stable flared frame designs. (Cross type shapes).

Some climbing sacks use removable, malleable, firm foam boards, which incorporate internal soft metal frames, which may then be moulded

Rucksacks

at will to fit your own personal back shape. A larger body contact area = increased stability for climbing.

Only by the early nineties does the problem seem to have been conquered. A bag that expands rather than a back that adjusts appears much more logical. With both shoulder strap and hip belt regions moving towards each other, or apart, the ideal location of the bags bulk, on the user's body, is constantly maintained, never becoming too low or too high. The constant ideal geometry is assured.

The advantages adjustable back systems offer include: Adjustment and versatility between summer and winter use, when wearing thick or thin clothing. Redistributing the load slightly while on the move. If you're a minority size, achieving a better fit.

It has been said that fixed back systems (no moving adjustability) are the better alternative. If it fits, it fits. (Many are available in different sizings). They also reduce any possibilities of failure as any moving parts pose more potential problems and incur more wear, particularly crucial when carrying the heaviest of loads. (Fixed backs are also cheaper to produce).

Many fixed back sacks offer the chance to remove the frames easily, enabling sacks to be rolled away or converted into soft packs. Some "adjustables" feature removable frames, to enable the fitting of replacement shoulder harnesses, but fixed varieties are generally easier to repair if necessary.

Ladies' bags are extremely popular, featuring rucksacks with back systems sized to suit a majority of women. Shorter back lengths, narrower tapered shoulder straps, (to avoid the bust line), scalloped hip belts (for traditional women's shape) and narrower take off points for shoulder straps (for narrower shoulders) all go to make sacks that have proved vastly more comfortable for many women.

HIP BELTS. (+ Body contact materials)

Resembling a broad and thick powerlifter's belt, the hip belt (or harness) and the lumbar region (found in the centre, attached directly to the base of the sack) are the key areas of weight dispersal. The better versions will usually be conical shaped and incorporate a stiffening board

69

of some form. (Usually plastic, polyproplene, or firm closed cell foam). This adds the strength necessary to spread the load over a larger area.

Obviously all belts are padded for comfort, but quality examples utilise a firm closed cell E.V.A foam structure, (as used in quality roll mats) as anything softer would soon collapse and flatten after little use. Often top of the range models will then cover this base with a softer open cell, more immediately comfortable, foam. This can also help stabilize the fit.

Suitable body contact materials should be used. More often than not a blend of polycotton (or similar e.g, polyester) is used. This is comfortable against the skin, or thin clothing, during the warmer months, offering durability, colour dyefastness, wickability and fast drying tendencies, while not being too abrasive in its own right, avoiding wearing holes in your clothing. Some manufacturers have developed their own exclusive materials, with anti-rot, high water resistance, high wear on folds and most notably, good friction (improving stability) being among the key claims.

The hardware of hip belts gives pride of place to the main hip belt buckle. Situated at the centre front, these buckles (always plastic = strong & lightweight; harder to freeze) feature some form of quick release mechanism. (No need to thread straps). The better type sport a kind of parachute release buckle design. With one simple clean movement, pulling back a flap, the buckle and belt quickly fall open; handy with cold or gloved hands.

Some belt designs will have the addition of slide buckles, enabling the user to relocate the main buckle to the most comfortable position. These are also used to neatly fasten away any surplus strapping.

On both sides, tucked away at the back of the belt, stabilising straps may sometimes be found. These travel from the outside of the belt's rear to the sides of the sack's main base and when tightened, help reduce any sideways swing.

But most importantly, good hip belts should feature good padding or careful shaping at the lumbar region.

SHOULDER STRAPS.

Unavoidably taking a little of the load, shoulder straps should really be regarded as stabilising features, simply stopping the bag from falling away from the user's back.

Obviously they should be padded and have comfortable contact fabrics, as described in the previous "hip belts" section, but their main improvements rest with their shaping. Precurved shoulder straps will sit, when curved over the top of your shoulders, in a comfortable tailored position. They should avoid digging in at the sides of your neck, while curving around neatly under/towards your arms.

The main adjustable straps tighten when you pull them in a backwards motion. A quality finishing feature involves the strap/webbing being stitched at intervals up the entire length of the shoulder strap. The buckle which attaches webbing to the main shoulder strap, can sometimes incorporate a curved, swivel type, feature, improving the comfort and automatic angling of the webbing's angle of travel. Loose strapping/ webbing ends sometimes feature a thumb loop. Not advised for safety reasons, this enables the user to relieve the weight of his arms, swinging sling-like on the ends of the straps.

One of the most important details of many shoulder straps is the use and presence of "top tensioning" straps. Situated at the top of the shoulders, attached from the shoulder strap to rucksack, these subtle items can make all the difference. Tightened so they are taut (the temptation is to over tighten them) they lift the top of the main strap off the user's shoulder slightly, transferring the weight from the top of the shoulder to the front of the arm. This can effectively eliminate aching shoulders and stabilize the entire carry. Crucial to their effectiveness is their position in relation to your shoulder. The strap's origin, from the sack, should sit approximately an inch above your shoulder line, but more importantly the point of shoulder takeoff should be directly at the top of your shoulder, from the highest point, to achieve the best results. (A small sliding buckle may offer you any necessary adjustment). Only in recent times has the simplest, but most brilliant, of details appeared, clarifying any confusion. A small pointer (small mark or colour flash) indicates where the strap should rest at the top of your shoulder. (Most important for adjustable back systems)

Such top tensioning straps can also offer a slight height adjustment for different sized backs, but usually offer most advantages for changes in terrain. When travelling up hill the straps can be loosened, allowing the sack to fall away from your back, remaining upright as you lean forward, while bumpy descents may require a tighter, more stabilising, setting.

Also as part of the rucksack's back, but showing the most variations, is the general middle-padded pressure pad section. This is the area catering for shoulder blades. Usually the design, utilising foam and contact materials, maintains, or gains, good air circulation around the small of the back. (Traditionally a problem area for over heating).

THE SACK'S BASIC DESIGN.

There are always variations, but generally all rucksacks today display the same basic design. A sack with a lid, two side pockets and a base compartment. (Exclude the side pockets for climbing sacks)

Lids usually use two quick release buckles and often incorporate an external or internal pocket. Lids with elastication offer a better fit, helping to repel the weather, while being able to pull far down over sacks only half full, or extend over sacks over packed. A few sacks feature extendable lids, which can increase capacity at will, while a handful of others, can detach and convert into small day sacks.

Weather closures, at the top of the sack's opening, underneath the lid, can be a very important detail. These are an extra circular piece of proofed fabric, (usually a thin nylon), which by the use of a central tightening drawcord partly or completely covers the top of the sack's contents. Slightly more elaborate versions may incorporate more fabric and an extra drawcord, sometimes called snow locks. (These can also allow loads to be packed higher)

Side pockets arrive in all sorts of guises, whether fixed, detachable or extendable. These days all close with zips, the better type using double pullers and travelling around the outside edge of the pocket, (zips start and finish pointing down) for easier access deeper inside, as opposed to skirting around the top edge and creating a lid. Pockets that fold away when not in use are handy, although a bit of a fiddle, while detachable pockets are popular but never as stable as permanent versions. Some people argue that pocketless sacks are more convenient (less cumbersome on trains and in thin crags, etc) but I find the many advantages of pockets

Rucksacks

far outweigh this slight disadvantage.

Some pockets may have loose channels at the rear, allowing tent poles and the like to slip down behind and strap to the outside of the sack; traditionally impossible with pocketed sacks.

On larger sacks, detachable pockets can sometimes be joined together to create smaller day sacks.

Base, or bottom, compartments form a separate chamber. (Often around 40% of the sack's overall volume). Usually only found on bags sized fifty litres and more, base compartments offer access to equipment through the bottom of the sack (via a zip) without having to sort through the kit situated at the top of the bag. (Particularly useful for storing sleeping bags, providing quick and easy access last thing at night).

The two independent chambers are segregated by a thin flap of nylon fabric, but virtually all dividers offer the open or closed option. Similar to weather closures at the top of the sack, the tightening or opening of a single drawcord (occasionally a zip) can convert the sack from a single chamber, to two separate compartments and back again. For anyone who might need to carry long items, such as tent poles, inside their sack, a small space/hole is nearly always left unstitched (usually in two corners) to allow the sack to be divided but still accommodate such items.

Access from the outside, via zips, is either through a straight or curved entry. Straight entries locate the zip running directly from one side of the sack's circumference to the other, splitting the sack, while curved varieties offer the easiest alternative as the zip creates a semi-circle shape at the front base of the bag. This creates a shape and flap allowing items to be easily lifted in or out.

Larger sacks will need the addition of two firmly tightened webbing straps (which open using Q/R buckles) fastening over such closures to avoid any weight straining the zip's teeth.

SACK FABRICS.

A sack is only as strong as its seams, but naturally a tough bag will be made from durable fabrics. The British are convinced that heavy texturised fabrics (coarse to the touch) are universally tougher than any other. This can often be the case, but surprisingly, many of the smoother fabrics provide much better and greater tear strengths.

Tear strength, rather than abrasion resistance, has a higher priority for rucksack construction. A rucksack's life is spent carrying heavy loads, which in turn put seams under a great and constant strain. While high quality of needle work pays dividends the inherent strength of a fabric's resistance to tearing, at these key areas, plays the greatest role. A fabric that wears and wears, but shows signs of tearing under strain where the needle has punctured its surface, is practically useless. More poor sacks are binned due to their tear resistance failing than any other reason. This is why most people's concern about a rucksack fabric's abrasion resistance should be supersede by inquiries about tear strengths. (Something not visually obvious).

As you might expect there are dozens of differing fabrics used for rucksacks in service today, all showing great improvements over the original canvas and cotton duck options. The two key materials used to create suitable modern fabrics revolve around nylon and polyester, each utilised in various deniers*. Whether 500 or 1000 denier, backed with nylon or coated with polyurethane, the options are vast, but all prominent and top quality manufacturers use suitable examples of both high abrasion and tear resistance strengths.

A typical example of a 1000 denier yarn, might be described as woven from a bulked nylon disarranged, looped and tangled (within it's bundle) filament yarn. By looping tangling and disarranging the yarns, greater strength is achieved, unusual with filament yarns and not usually found in traditional and conventional industrially spun yarns.

(*Denier = weight/thickness of yarn. The higher the denier number = heavier/thicker the yarn. 9000 metres of a yarn weighing 1 grams = 1 denier).

The "Martindale test", is the commercial test for measuring abrasion resistance. A flat sample of fabric is subjected to constant abrasion, but in actual use (stitched together in the form of a rucksack) the results can be misleading as the performance of most textiles is reduced when folded edges are exposed. e.g, at seams, which is also the location on a sack commonly in contact with abrasive rock, etc.

Rucksacks

Some fabrics laid flat can withstand forty-eight times the amount an identical sample, exposing a folded edge, can endure before wearing through. Some manufacturers independently test fabrics under such conditions.

Some smooth, closely woven, fabrics, while under strong pressure, have yarns jet blown while spun to achieve incredible strengths, while others deliberately create softer weaves to help deflect any glancing blows. Fabric construction does seem to be one area where manufacturers often disagree, but some general rules and guide lines follow. (All relate to quality versions)

The finer the weave, the higher the tear strength. (Not tightly woven. Loosely threaded fabric causes threads to lock together and slow/stop a tear).

The higher the denier, (opposite to fine weave) the better the abrasion resistance. (Although some are backed with coatings to improve tear strength).

The lower the denier the more supple a fabric becomes, while keeping the overall sack weight to a minimum.

To increase waterproofing (details to follow) more polyurethane backing (most common example) is required. The higher the hydrostatic head (improved waterproofing) the stiffer the fabric, which reduces the abrasion residence on a fold.

WATERPROOF.

Virtually all rucksack fabrics today are waterproof but few sacks can actually claim to be. Fabrics are produced to be waterproof, but seams remain a potential (and eventually likely) area for water penetration. Unlike waterproof clothing, due to constant stretching and straining of heavy loads, which rucksacks have to endure, rucksack seams cannot be taped. Water proof fabrics will keep contents dry through showers, but for any prolonged period of wet weather, ultimately the only real satisfactory solution is the internal use of a large plastic bag. (There are more elaborate and stronger bags, or covers, made specifically for this purpose. You may also try using tent seam sealant).

In 1978 the world's first waterproof, texturised, fabric, KS-100e, was developed and launched by the Lancashire manufacturer, Karrimor. The 100 represented the height, in cms, the fabric achieved under hydrostatic head tests. (= didn't leak under continuous 100cm high column of water). To improve its handle and tear strength an additional elastomeric coating was applied. Some fabrics have hydrophobic finishings on the outside to increase resistance against grease and oil contamination. Seams are responsible for a sack's true strength. On quality sacks all main seams are usually stitched over their internal edges. This obviously strengthens them, but also adds extra degrees of weather protection. On some poorer examples of sacks, take away a single line of stitching and the whole base will fall through. Some manufacturers may boast of the use of high grade nylon threads.

"I know the fabric's waterproof, but is it breathable?"

BUCKLES AND STRAPS.

Straps, or webbing, on sacks may be made from polypropylene mixtures but nylon is most commonly preferred due to it's extra strength, abrasion resistance and higher resistance to UV light degradation. (All modern examples of strapping don't freeze or rot).

Better qualities of plastic type buckles and sliders are produced from nylon 66. (occasionally Delrin). Any buckles that regularly need to be opened always feature quick release designs. (The depression of two areas, simultaneously, instantly opens the device and allows reclosing without having to adjust the webbing lengths). Some buckles can be brutally bent and mauled without inflicting harm.

Rucksacks

Many of these buckles and accessories are available separately as spare parts, although, cunningly, few brands are interchangeable.

RUCKSACK CAPACITIES.

All sacks' capacities and volumes are measured in litres. 75 and 65 litres (nearly always displayed on, or as part of the sack's name) were the most common and popular sizes, until the advances in the lightweight equipment promoted the latter in popularity. There seem to be larger and smaller versions of bags claiming the same litreage capacity, as these measurements usually appear to be approximate, only serving to offer rough guide lines. Rather than choosing a size you think you need, choose a size you think you can carry. (Incidentally, unless you're fanatical enough to saw the handle off your tooth brush, I find concerns about differing weights of the actual sacks themselves, rather extreme.)

THE RIGHT FIT OF A RUCKSACK.

Obviously one indication of a correctly fitting sack is general comfort, but to achieve this:

Weight on hips. (Some ladies' sacks may rest better around the waist). Shoulder straps shouldn't slip off shoulders. (Consider chest straps). Top tension straps should rest around an inch above the shoulder line. The webbing will often take a 25 degree angle. Shoulder straps shouldn't yield much weight.

When wearing the sack, you shouldn't need to lean too far forward.

REGULAR FEATURES.

While the massive extent of sacks produced world-wide create an inexhaustible amount of varying details, the following is a list, with explanations, of the most commonplace and classic features regularly found on most sacks today.

Side compression straps.

Usually featuring on sacks without side pockets, two straps running horizontally across both sides of a sack can offer a number of advantages. Sometimes used to attach side pockets, side compression straps are usually tools enabling the general size and volume of a sack to be reduced while also stabilising its contents. The best example is stabilising half loads. Rather than have contents of a half filled sack crashing around at its base, also providing a poor carry and line of gravity, the tightening of these side adjustments spreads the load in a thinner and upright form. This helps create a stable load and improve the carry.

In conjunction with other attachments, these straps are often used for attaching various pieces of climbing equipment. Most notably in conjunction with wand pockets (two small open pockets on both sides of the base) they can be used to carry tent poles or skis. (The pockets stop poles, etc, from sliding down and through. Some wand pockets feature hidden slits, enabling long skis to exit through the bottom. The skis are then tied at the top). Wand pockets should incorporate drainage eyelets.

Haul Loops.

Always situated in between the two shoulder straps at the top of a sack, this is the only and most convenient point from which to haul a fully laden rucksack. (Often bar tacked). Manhandling heavy sacks from any other attachments (excluding shoulder straps) can often result in damage. For climbers, this is also where ropes for hauling up sacks, should be attached.

Chest Straps.

For many these can make the world of difference. Fixtures on some sacks, but also available separately, these adjustable and removable chest harnesses can either help stabilise a sack, or more commonly, eliminate shoulder strap slippage. (A particular problem with narrow shoulders).

Ice Axe Loops.

Nobody is sure why, but all medium and large sacks display ice axe loops. (Sometimes two. Sometimes adjustable). Obviously for transporting ice axes, they can also be used for carrying some walking sticks. (Slide the sharp end of the axe down through the bottom loop, swing/lift the same end directly up and fasten in the top adjustable strap). Crampon straps are also occasionally found on rucksack lids, hopefully not too close to the rear of the carrier's head.

Bottom Carry Straps.

Two handy straps for fastening long equipment externally. (Tents or roll mats. Not sleeping bags; keep those inside). There are many variations of these designs but all serve the same purpose.

Lid Compression Strap.

Occasionally found inside the top lid, over weather locks/closures, these tighten and compress the sack at this bulging area.

Accessory Patches.

Plastic patches which provide the opportunity to attach extra equipment via the use of straps.

CARE.

There isn't a lot you can do to care for your sack, other than avoid mishaps. Some saddlers may help, and there are some specific rucksack repair services, but many quality manufacturers will make repairs to your sack (their own brand) for a small fee. Some manufacturers shout about it, but most better brands are "Lifetime guaranteed", as usually all materials and workmanship are guaranteed against defects. (This does not cover misuse and the natural breakdown and ageing, through use)

When travelling abroad by plane, it can be an idea to place your sack inside a simple plastic bag, as this will ensure that baggage handlers will throw the pack around, as a whole, and not by pulling on (often pulling off) a single strap or flap.

It's virtually impossible to lock rucksacks (thieves will only slash fabric anyhow) but some movement alarms are available. Some travellers, destined for dubious countries, go through the trouble of lining their sacks with chicken wire, foiling any attempt to cut and steal from the sack.

Note that "all-green" sacks may be unwise in certain parts of the world as associations with military use can occur.

When out in the field, strong carpet tape can internally repair cuts and tears in a sack's fabric.

(See page 82 for manufacturer's listings & details)

DAY SACKS.

To avoid repeating much of the information covered in "Rucksacks", (fabric, contact materials, etc) the following section is merely additional.

A Day sack is what you should use to manage all those pieces of equipment and accessories you find useful and necessary to accompany you on walks of any distance. The bag, being a small version of a larger rucksack, will not only make walking a lot easier and more enjoyable but adds the safety element of leaving your hands free.

No longer called Knapsacks, Day sacks have been promoted from green canvas hanging bags, with leather straps and metal buckles, to often offer just as much thought and design as their larger relatives. Much of the modern design owes its improvement to the larger versions as their features and knowledge have trickled down, providing the majority with quick release plastic buckles, comfortable colour dyefast body contact fabrics (which line the back and insides of shoulder straps), waist belts, chest harnesses and waterproof highly robust, but lightweight, fabrics.

Of all the thousands of varying designs, shapes and colours, most Day sacks use the same proven design; a bag with a lid and two shoulder straps. I always feel that Day sacks are among the easiest self-service part of a walker's kit. Generally, what you see is what you get. Different qualities of manufacturer and materials will always be reflected in the price, but some key features to look out for and consider are as follows.

Size. Day sack size is measured in litreage. (How many litres of fluid each bag could hold). Usually starting from around as little as 16 litres, they generally go up to 45, although some walkers have used 50. If there's one mistake anyone's ever made when buying a Day sack, it's buying it too small. Countless people look at stuffed up sacks on a shop wall and optimistically underrate the extent of their day kit, or rather overrate the size of the bag. "Oh yes, that should be plenty big enough", is the common quote from a Day sack shopper. Too often their

Rucksacks

idealistic hopes outweigh the realities of how much room a set of waterproofs, a sandwich box, steel flask, camera and all other sorts of knick-knacks we only remember as we pack, actually take up in volume. One problem a hopeful person might have is to settle with a bag that always only just manages to squeeze everything in, under a bursting lid. It's never nice to have to carry your jumper over your shoulder, as you inevitably heat up and reduce your clothing. Having extra space in the sack will avoid this. Obviously an over-large bag can result in not only annoyingly swinging about upon your back, but also inflicting a nasty blow to the head of a stile climbing rambler.

Many bags, for more adventurous activities such as climbing and mountain cross cycling, incorporate features to compress the contents of a half filled bag. Providing a chest harness will also help to tighten the fit, reduce any swing and avoid shoulder straps sliding off narrow shoulders.

While a neatly and evenly packed larger rucksack is a necessary requirement for a good, safe and comfortable load, Day sacks rarely acquire enough weight to cause concern.

My personal recommendation would be not to consider anything smaller than a 30 - 35 litre sack, especially if carrying for two, as it's surprising how quickly smaller bags fill up.

Shape. Long thin Day sacks with no side pockets are either a genuine climbing sack, designed to carry a load best suited for climbers or a Day sack of European origin or influence. This style seems to be increasingly in demand in Britain, though if you stop any of its supporters and ask why they prefer it, most are unable to tell you. Perhaps they prefer the look? Fair enough, but the vast majority of U.K walkers still prefer a bag with side pockets. Not having to fumble to the bottom of your bag for that last camera film or chocolate bar seems sensible.

Pockets. Side pockets are useful, but the common thought that they should be large enough to accommodate a flask, I feel, is unfair and not a good idea in the first place. The pockets should be zipped for secure closure, preferably around the top edge of the pocket, with the zip's start and finish pointing down, like a flap off the side, enabling access more easily than a zip that starts from the main body of the bag and travels across and around the top of the pocket, like a lid.

Different bags will further offer extra and varying pocket designs, usually at the front and on the lid. Look out for the useful hidden security pockets often found on the inside of the top lid, regularly found on more deluxe models.

The back. The back of the bag should carry the main weight of concern as, along with the shoulder straps, it is the main contact area with yourself. Many Day sacks are still available with soft backs; that is, backs with no padding. Some people prefer this, as being able to roll the bag up entirely can be an advantage, although a bag with some form of foam and back padding will offer more comfort.

In recent times nearly all manufacturers have incorporated a series of stitch lines and patterns into and across padded backs, alas, barely increasing air circulation but merely highlighting the fact that they are padded. Such pattern details can be ignored.

Some designs settle simply for a piece of close cell, bubble type material, slipped inside a loose pocket on the inside of the back, which can usually be removed, providing either a completely soft bag or a handy mat.

Some designers have cleverly incorporated the added strength and stiffness of a preformed and moulded padded back to hold a particularly suitable shape, ideally leaving a percentage of your own back untouched and free to breathe.

Shoulder Straps. Their design is obviously of importance for carrying comfort. It's nearly impossible to find any that are unpadded. For extra comfort some are curved (curving outwards, at the bottom, when held flat), enabling them to nestle neatly around your shoulders.

The amount of webbing/strap should be ample enough for you to loosen and enlarge the slack for occasions when wearing a thicker coat or jacket. Observe how close their birth is from the sack, as this might prove uncomfortable for a broad shouldered man. The simplest and best way of being sure is to try it on.

Nice finishing features include both webbing straps and buckle anchor points, to travel, stitched occasionally, up the full length of

Rucksacks

padded shoulder straps and into the top of the bag; this reduces the dangers of pulling away or ripping. A more important detail is for the connecting piece of webbing/strap, stitched and anchored to the bottom of the sack, to be neatly tailored into a triangular protruding piece of fabric. This spreads the pulling force over a larger area and number of stitches, again reducing the risk of straps pulling out of seams. A plastic buckle stitched and anchored to the main shoulder strap at a suitable angle can also enhance a fit.

More unusual are small bags that open and close through a zip system, which enables a larger area of the bag to opened at any one time. Useful for lifting items straight out, but zips have moving parts and always pose a source of unreliability. (They can also freeze up in triple-point weather conditions).

Waist belt. These belts are a very practical feature, particularly for larger bags, as they eliminate any up and down bouncing movement. Usually a simple 25mm wide strap and a single quick release buckle is all that's necessary, but users should avoid confusion with padded hip belts. A waist belt simply reduces the sack's movement, holding it steady and usually sitting, not around the hips, but around the waist.

MANUFACTURERS. The following is a short list of only some rucksack labels of note...

Karrimor: With a history of rucksack manufacturing, dating back to the late fifties, Karrimor are a major player in the international rucksack league, constantly sustaining their high status. With their quality setting standards, their large range should have something to offer everyone. Brilliant.

Berghaus are a world class manufacturer of rucksacks, with some great designs to their credit. With excellent quality, there's no such thing as a bad Berghaus sack. Innovators and pioneers of "ladies' sacks", Berghaus have a basic quality and standard hard to match.

Lowe Alpine manufactured in Ireland, Lowe produce excellent rucksacks. Their comfort, construction and reliability are particularly good..

Other notable names include: Vaude, Northface, Jack Wolfskin, Macpac.

Other brands that offer good value, and many economy options include: Vango, Freeman, Freetime, Llewelyn Wynne.

TENTAGE

- Ensure you are using the correct product.
- Read all instructions carefully prior to use.
- **DO NOT** proof items which are dirty.
- **DO NOT** use detergents when cleaning and rinse thoroughly afterwards.
- Protect grass and tarmac.
- Use a new brush or spray where possible.
- Apply the proofing thoroughly, panel by panel but be careful not to over apply.
- **DO NOT** splash proofing on tent windows.
- **DO NOT** proof tents when damp or wet.
- After use, always dry tents carefully and store in a safe place away from damp.

CLOTHING

- Ensure you are using the correct product.
- Read all instructions carefully prior to use.
- **DO NOT** proof items which are dirty.
- **DO NOT** use detergents when cleaning and rinse thoroughly afterwards.
- When using Super-Pel always tumble dry or iron.
- Allow clothing to dry thoroughly before use.
- Remember - Super-Pel is concentrated - 100ml will treat 1kg of clothing.
- Always look after garments which have been proofed when not in use.
- Super-Pruf is suitable for GORE-TEX® lined clothing.

FOOTWEAR

- Ensure you are using the correct product.
- Read all instructions carefully prior to use.
- **DO NOT** proof dirty footwear.
- **DO NOT** clean with detergents.
- Where possible allow footwear to dry naturally.
- Ensure total thorough coverage.
- **DO NOT** over apply waxes.
- Don't forget - you can polish G-WAX to a shine if required.
- Don't forget to seal welts if necessary.
- G-SPORT is suitable for all GORE-TEX® lined footwear.

Please Remember - All Grangers products are ready to apply without any pre-treatment, and have an unlimited shelf life.

	FABSIL	FABSIL SPRAY / FABSIL GOLD	NYLOPRUF	MESOWAX	SUPER-PEL	G-SPORT	G-WAXCREAM / G-WAX SPRAY	MAXOL	SUPERPRUF	MAPDRY
COTTON CANVAS	●	●						●		
POLYCOTTON		●						●		
NYLON		●	●					●		
BREATHABLE FABRICS					●	●		●	●	
POLYESTERS		●			●			●		
ACRYLICS		●			●			●		
LEATHER				●	●	●	●			
SUEDE						●		●		
WOOL					●					
PAPER										●

*GORE-TEX is a Registered Trade Mark of W.L. Gore & Associates Inc.

GENERAL CLOTHING.

What is the best clothing and the best combination of clothing? Often it's personal preference, what you get on best with, which will usually take a lot of experimenting to arrive at. What type of clothing you choose can also be dictated by what type of walking you engage in and what types of terrain and weather you're likely to encounter.

Traditionally, for general walking, your domestic wardrobe could cater for outdoor demands, such as thick woollen jumpers and tweed trousers. Hopefully this can still be the case, but now there are a dozen or more modern alternatives to every piece of traditional clothing.

In this chapter we take a look at what modern designs and science offer us today.

LAYERING.

Almost a cliche, but wearing layers is the best solution to walking discomforts. Most people's dissatisfaction with their clothing is usually due to overheating or not being warm enough, wanting to be cool when it's hot and warm when it's not.

Whether with traditional clothing or modern products, various layers offer more options to control our own varying climate. (Modern clothing is designed as part of an overall layering system). More thin layers, rather than fewer thick ones, improve our temperature control over periods when extra exertion might increase our warmth, or changing weather conditions may influence our comfort. Layers are our tools for heat regulation.

An obvious example of this can be when walking in the cooler months. Starting out, extra warm clothing compensates for cooler conditions but very quickly our bodies may warm up and begin to overheat. Not only is this uncomfortable, but in some winter conditions can be dangerous as surplus perspiration can accelerate heat loss. The person wearing layers can peel layers off, but the person wearing a thick duvet, for example, removes too much, or nothing at all.

When out walking always remember that the way to keep warm is to stay cool. British mountaineer, Winthrop-Young, summed it up when he wrote; "The way to stay warm in the mountains is not to get hot".

However, while the simple layering strategy is easily adopted, its basic logic can be improved. Use layers, **but choose the right layers.** The basic principles of what different layers should achieve are simple. They can be simplified into three parts;

1. The first layer, next to the skin, or base layer. Too many people confuse this area of clothing with thermals, designed to keep you warm, but people should be re-educated in regarding this important area as a comfort layer.

It is true that most of the best products and materials for this layer are referred to as "thermal", but the same science that keeps you warm also helps to keep you cool in the summer. The base layer's main duty is to wick (transport) perspiration away from the wearer's skin. The moisture that sits around on you skin in cold conditions turns cold quickly, inducing it's chilling effects. As it dries it steals your heat; disastrous when trying to keep warm. A good base avoids this. Excess moisture in the warmer months is absorbed and wicked away by good base layers which simultaneously draw off excess heat, helping to keep you cool.

Modern thermals are excellent (more to follow) but, surprising to some walkers, a polycotton material is far better than cotton alone. Pure cotton quickly absorbs too much perspiration and tends to hold on to it, acting like a blotting paper. This is very uncomfortable and is often confused with why a breathable waterproof is, apparently, not working. Polycotton reserves the pleasurable comfort of cotton but improves the wicking action (drying quicker) of plain polyester.

2. The second, middle, layer. (Or mid-layer). Sometimes known as the warmth layer, it is indeed concerned with warmth. This can be easily achieved with many methods and materials, but again, importantly, it should be able to effectively continue the wicking away

of moisture. Ideally, moisture should travel continuously on to and out through the third outer layer.

General Clothing

3. The outer, or shell, layer. The shell should protect you and your inner layers from the affects of the wind or rain, also protecting you from the wind chill factor. For full details of the most common and usual shells, see the Waterproofs chapter. Less obvious these days, but common once, were garments purely acting as a wind-break. These, usually cotton, outer jackets (often shower proofed and now referred to as trekking jackets) are still available and used, but the advent of waterproof/ breathable garments and windproof fleeces (more to follow) has gone a long way to discontinue such items. Plus the disadvantages of carrying two garments; one waterproof (non-breathable) and one windproof.

UNDERSTANDING MORE ABOUT CLOTHING

As clothing choices are often a personal consideration, understanding what materials do what, quickly helps your knowledge of what's required and best avoided.

Natural cellulose fibres. = from plants. e.g, cotton, linen.

Natural protein fibres. = from animals. e.g, wool, leather, silk.

Artificial cellulose fibres. = from wool pulp. e.g, rayon, cellophane.

Artificial noncellulonic fibres. = from petroleum, coal, etc. e.g, nylon, polyester, polypropylene.

The following is a selection of basic materials and fabrics:

Cotton. A popular and, in general use, comfortable material. (Especially next to the skin). A good insulator against both cold and heat when dry; unfortunately, in cold conditions when wet it freezes hard and insulation discontinues. Cotton's thirst for moisture however, in hot weather can have beneficial effects; good for hot climate trekking/ travelling/walking. (For long distance travelling, cotton can mildew if left damp). Tightly woven it becomes windproof.

Wool. Too easily written off by modern activists, wool can be a marvellous material to wear. Its tightly curled fibres trap air effectively, creating warmth, while remaining supple, stretchy and, most of all, warm when wet. When totally saturated and waterlogged, it can still offer half its original insulation value. A two part fibre, its inner core absorbs water, while its outer membrane repels it, which is how evaporated body moisture is also safely transported away from the wearer. Similar to many modern thermal fibres. (See Thermals section)

Wool however feels uncomfortable against the skin, has low durability and tears easily. The latter complaints are often remedied by the introduction of synthetic (e.g. nylon) materials incorporated within the wool's blend.

(You can effectively proof wool, for improved drying, with products available from walking/camping stores).

Silk. Silk fibres boast the highest strength to weight ratio of all natural fibres. Like wool, it offers highly efficient insulation even when considerably wet, yet unlike wool it is comfortable against the skin. It can stretch up to 20% over it's relaxed state, helping to make it particularly favoured for unrestrictive underwear. However, silk isn't cheap and is weakened by strong sunlight, ironing, and perspiration.

Polyester. Often best used in conjunction with other materials. Polyester is both strong and durable but also unexpensive. Appearing as late as the forties, its origin is similar to nylon but was considered vastly inferior until it evolved into such strains as Dacron, Hollow fibres for insulation, soft outer fabrics for laminates, micro fibres, polypropylene and perhaps most notably, fleece. (See, Fleeces, to follow) Mixed with cotton, it also reduces the fabric's weight. Distant cousins include; vinyl, acrylic and neoprene.

Acrylic. Used to describe numerous acrylonitrile fibres. Cheap, it often appears in economy sleeping bags, but usually used mixed with wool or as thermal unders. Used for economy.

Polyproplene. An Italian invention, its soft (yet durable) handling and cheap petroleum-based chemistry make it popular for carpets and ropes. Norwegians discovered how to produce it in fine textiles and by the eighties the word "polypro" was on the lips of many outdoor enthusiasts. (Tradenames include: Montefibre, Meraklon).

Its refusal to absorb any moisture make it apt at wicking away moisture at great speed, which is effective at eliminating perspiration evaporating

General Clothing

off the skin. When worn, as it absorbs no water, it dries rapidly. As discussed in the "Base layer", of the layering principals, polypropylene is effective at helping to avoid the cooling effects of perspiration evaporation, which is important for keeping warm in cold conditions, but is not a good insulation material.

Disadvantages include, delicate requirements of care, odours, melting at high temperatures (ironing), pilling and is difficult to dry when soaked. However, this forerunner of all synthetic "next to the skin" materials, is very comfortable in use.

Nylon. It's cheap, easy to treat (coatings), abrasion resistant, durable, stronger than cotton, dries quickly, usually windproof and is difficult to rot. On the negative side, ultraviolet light can eventually weaken it, rain and water can stretch it (a problem for nylon tents) and edges can easily fray. (There are further details of nylon characteristics in the "Tents" chapter) Not cheap but some forms can be re-heated and stretched, similar to tensile steel.

Quickly becoming a classic material by the early forties, nylon was introduced by Du Pont, who consequently failed to trademark and register the name. As a result it almost simultaneously became a generic word for other materials also produced from polymers. From these various fibres stem the multitude of various nylon fabrics. Including...

Taffeta. An extremely common and relatively cheap nylon fabric. It has decent abrasion resistance and for nylon is quiet. Used for tents, sleeping bags, cheap waterproofs, to laminated waterproofs, although in the latter region its use has drastically declined.

Ripstop. Within its weave a distinctive checkered pattern exists. (Occasional vertical and horizontal threads are doubled). This helps halt the progress of tears. This technique can also be used to reduce fabric weights while maintaining overall strength. (Durable coatings can reduce its "rip-stopping" feature). Ideal for sleeping bags, totally contradictory to original perceptions, it's now often used in clothing and waterproofs. (Ripstop cotton is also used for clothing). The Japanese produce particularly soft and pleasant versions.

Taslan. In quality waterproofs, an extremely common fabric and often overlooked as a nylon due to its slight textured finish. Each yarn is spun within a jet of air (air bulked) leaving it with a rough texture. When tightly woven it still feels smooth, but tough. Indeed taslan is extremely tough, abrasion resistant, strong, yet also light and supple.

Cordura. (A Du Pont fabric. There are many similar versions). The monster of nylons, its rough and large weave make it the most abrasion resistant, tear resistant and durable. Originally developed for car tyres, unfortunately it is often too heavy and stiff for many applications, although different deniers exist. (Denier = weight/thickness of yarn)

The list of nylon materials is vast but others include; Cambrelle (usually a boot lining), Pack cloth, Ballistics cloth.

Lycra. A stretch material, famous for cycling and running shorts. Used occasionally on walker's kit to trim cuffs and hems and mixed with other fibres to provide extra stretch. (E.g, "Spandura", A Cordura and lycra mix, a virtually indestructible stretch fabric. "Spandura 2": a knitted, 160 denier yarn, stretchy and durable, but soft, cheaper and lighter version. Both used for breeches, etc.)

Microfibres. There are dozens of these modern fabrics, which have quickly spread in popularity in almost every area of kit. Synthetic materials create these dense but lightweight (often extremely thin) fabrics, which offer windproofing, small packsize, durability, featherweight suppleness, rapid drying and high rain resistance. (With a suitable coating, also waterproof). Their secret lies with the tightness of their ultra fine filaments. (Teflon coatings improve their durability).

Mixtures. Many materials are often combined to unite favourable features, or combat disadvantages. Polycotton is a classic example. Another occasional description of a hybrid is tagged, 60/40. This blends 60% cotton running top to bottom, while the other 40% of nylon threads run horizontally. This greatly improves the strength of plain cotton, making it common in lightweight walking trousers. Another, less common, version includes 65/35. All threads are 65% polyester encased, or wrapped, in cotton. This improves the comfort of plain polyester threads.

(Warp thread = vertical thread. Weft = horizontal)

General Clothing

FLEECES. (Synthetic, fluffy type garments)

A description of a general modern fleece and what it offers would be: The warmth of two or more jumpers, in one lightweight flexible layer. They dry quickly, compared to wool are many times harder wearing, lighter weight, have higher windproof standards, are easy to wash and are comfortable against the skin. Originally a next to the skin, or over thermals, layer, fleece now happily serves as an outer layer too, but definitively would be described as a mid-layer.

Fleeces now play a major part in the walking wardrobe and play a substantial role in the turnover of may walking and camping retailers. Surprising statistics of just how many walking families now own a fleece show the quickest and most recent explosion of success now selling by the thousand, usually for no better use than propping up the local bar. A constant source of conversation within the trade is " when will the fleece bubble burst?"

Originally, manufacturers of rucksacks, tents, or waterproofs, were looking for something to keep their machinists busy during the quieter production months. Making a few fleece garments seemed a simple answer, but to everyone's surprise this moonlighting quickly overtook much of the overall production schedule. The public had never seen the like of such fabrics, fleeces were a radical new item of clothing. Often palmed off as "fashionable", manufacturers finally got their hands on something that could sustain healthy mark ups and help upgrade the trade's general image. Even the high street fashion stores have tried to cash in on the party, but with no success. (It is a genuine fact that quality fleeces have successfully been reserved for specialist outdoor leisure shops).

Essentially an Everest standard of product, fleeces are popular for many activities. Often they are genuinely practical, but it's interesting just how many of the public have absorbed the blurb that fleece is simply brilliant for everything, with people rarely stopping to ask, "is it?" I own two or three fleeces, which serve well for many occasions, but I much prefer the use of a quality wool jumper for lounging around the house. In that instance, fleece, with typical cuffs and hems, I find uncomfortable.

Fleeces are a strange product, in the sense that their name is used to describe a product, while also the material. Do we call a cotton shirt, a "cotton?" It's usually understood that a "fleece" describes a standard design of jacket. i.e, hip length, with zip and hip collar, usually with two pockets. The many variations of fleece garment designs are endless, but I've always found the simplest truly cash in on the nature of the product and material. Manufacturers should perhaps, more often, design fleeces around the material, rather than a garment that is then made from fleece.

(Fleece is also used for hats, gloves, scarfs, mitts, etc).

Returning to the possible origins of fleece clothing, we must return to fibrepile, originally used by Norwegian fishermen. The name is quite descriptive as essentially its a collection of synthetic fibres manipulated to produce a dense but soft layer of fine loops; effective at trapping air, = warmth.

For half the weight, fibrepile supplies the same warmth as wool, but unlike wool absorbs next to no water. This enables it to dry quickly and wick moisture well. Still popular and in use by many, fibrepile is durable, lightweight and compared with more recent materials, cheap. Unfortunately, fibrepile isn't comfortable against the skin and tends to quickly pill.

Through the seventies various types and brands evolved, but most are now unavailable or unheard of. The most common pile available today is nylon pile. Similar to modern fleece, but using a locked stitching, it's lighter than most standard-weight fleeces of comparable warmth.

The first products that came along, which encourage the term "fleece", were similar to thicker sweatshirts. (Fleece originally referred to thinner pile). Polyester filaments were woven in a flat layer; one side smooth, the other, thousands of loose strands which were tucked back into the fabric.

True fleece, as we know it today, arrived in earnest with Polarfleece. (By Malden Mills). Made from 100% Dacron, Du pont polyester, the fabric trapped cold air in the outer surface, while retaining body warmth in the inner layer; achieved by tucking and double napping the polyester strands on both sides. While having low permeability,

General Clothing

dissipating wind, it also displayed a comfortable and pleasant feel, with most of the practical advantages offered by pile. Although it was pushed as an aesthetically pleasing product the reality was that it pilled badly. (Bubbling up, quickly looking jaded and tatty). Practically, it performed excellently, but a non-pilling version needed to be introduced (sacrificing windproofing) to satisfy the public's desire for smartness.

Polarplus, a double-faced velour pile, was the result and what most fleeces are now based on. (Originally introduced as "Synchilla").

Most fleeces are knitted, with loops on one side, from polyester. Basically, large industrial rolling brushes fluff it up. More brushing = more or thicker pile. It's appearance is trimmed, sheared over and smartened up before a heat treatment stretches it to any required widths.

There are a number of manufacturers producing good fleece fabrics but undoubtedly the market is dominated by Malden Mills, producers of, amongst others, Polartec, Polarlite and Polarplus. (now known as Polartec 100, 200 & 300). Various clothing manufacturers buy these fabrics and with them produce their own garments and designs. At one time describing the differences in fleeces was simple. Thin, thicker and even thicker, relating to their warmths, was all we need know, but in recent times fleeces have been nurtured and developed to establish more options offering various performance and advantages. It's now arguable whether choosing a fleece is as simple as choosing what ever colour or style takes our fancy.

"Any garment with a shiny liner, is windproof", was the type of expression used to describe fleeces with a windproof lining. Using fleece in conjunction with other fabrics is an extension of the subject. More to follow.

To avoid vagueness, the following is a brief rundown of most fleece types:

Polartec 100. A thinner, knitted, non-brushed, fleece originally intended as an underwear weight.

Polartec 100M. The same microdenier fleece with an added finish. Ideal as a warmer base layer, or midweight mid-layer.

93

Polartec 110. Lightweight, (thinner than 200) one-way stretch fleece.

Polartec 4. Similar to 110, brushed on one side only, it's as warm, but has improved moisture wicking properties. Its non-brushed, knitted side (worn outwards) spreads moisture over a larger area to help evaporation.

Polartec 200. Probably the most common and popular of all fleeces, it's a good general all round performer. (Made from Dacron II polyester = lightweight - 267g/m2. Formerly Polarlite, it's now brushed on both sides)

Polartec 200S. With an added 10% of Lycra providing a four-way stretch.

Polartec 200PS. (Power Stretch) Also with a four-way lycra stretch, it has low weight but high insulation. The outer side has a nylon face = non-pilling and abrasion resistant. The inner face is a low bulk fast wicking velour/pile.

Polartec 200DWR. Standard 200 treated with a "Durable Water Repellency".

Polartec 200/3D. Slightly thicker than standard 200, it features compressed and heat-applied aesthetic patterns. Said to have better resistance to pilling.

Polartec lite. A cross between Polortec 100 and 200.

Polartec 300. Thicker than Polartec 200, a fleece for colder conditions or low activity.

Polartec 300W. Features an external aesthetic wool type finish and offers durability, while maintaining its appearance. (Although not as soft).

Polartec 200 & 300 Recycled. Recycled fleece. See "Green Clothing" section.

Polartec Windbloc series. Non-pill velour pile (with DWR), laminated on both sides of a breathable/windproof polyurethane barrier, producing a tough totally windproof fleece fabric.

General Clothing

Synchilla. Another brand name for Polartec fleeces by Malden Mills.

Sportant. A dense, abrasion resistant, but soft, fleece.

Thermovelour. Similar to a durable Polartec 200.

Tritec. Waterproof fleece, incorporating a hydrophilic stretch membrane, inside two layers of fleece. Versions using fleece on only one side, allow seams to be taped = waterproof garment.

Aquafleece. Also waterproof due to an inner membrane sandwiched inside.

Ultra fleece (Or Karisma): This thin and lightweight contender (Terinda fibres are woven, not knitted) claims to dry faster than any other fleece, is more windproof than several; jumpers (and considerably more than other standard fleeces), is also unbelievably durable, truly anti-pilling and no longer suffers from the annoying "clinging to the fingers" touch. Non-stretch, but underrated.

Ultifleece: As a traditional thickness of fleece this double sided "Tactel" claims to be three times more wind resistant than other standard fleeces.

Doufold's own fleece, claims to be the first of the laminated windproof type. Stretch waterproof polyurethane is laminated in between two layers of single-sided microfibre fleece.

When wearing fleeces, not as a mid-layer but as an outer layer, a key problem for some users is that most are far from windproof. If wearing a fleece purely for increased warmth, a 10 mph wind could reduce the wearer's skin temperature to 15c. (A windproof liner could maintain warmth at over 23c)

"Well, it's nice to have fleeced you sir".

A solution by many clothing manufacturers is to accompany some of their fleeces with a windproof liner, or shell, often offering a reversible option. This offers good versatility for temperature control. Protecting the fleece on the inside obviously improves it's warmth. A common fabric used is "Perex", also being lightweight and fast drying. (Such lightweight, windproof, inners or outers can be bought separately).

W.L. Gore (producers of Gore-tex fabric) have produced their own version of windproof fabric to solve the problem. It claims to be windproof, while particularly breathable, but I find the biggest advantage, by coincidence, is its pleasant warm touch on bare skin when wearing a short sleeved shirt. It can also be laminated in between two layers of fleece.

Fleece garments, worn over undergarments, with smooth windproof linings are far easier to pull on and off, and can reduce restriction of movement.

Windproof fleeces however can be limited in versatility, as they can become too warm. Non-windproof fleeces offer a form of air conditioning.

For a long time (and still popular) the facility to "zip-in" a fleece inside your waterproof jacket was a major selling pitch. Admittedly the idea of physically combining the two to make an instant winter garment appeals, but is usually impractical. Sure, use and seek this feature for the occasional day to day use, but personally, for walking, I

General Clothing

find it unnecessary and a hindrance. Reasons include: When the fleece is zipped inside your outer garment (using two internal zips either side of the outer jacket's main zip), you leave a two inch gap, running your full length, uninsulated, ironically directly behind the zip. The sleeves, etc, still pull out independently. Your perfect fitting fleece, once zipped inside the second garment, takes on a new fitting (often uncomfortable) as its natural line and drape has been altered. (Especially around the collar).

You never see professional mountaineers using such systems. They recognize the failings and much prefer the more effective independent use of a fleece, in its own right, simply worn underneath their outer shell.

The various physical design features of fleece garments are numerous, but quite obvious on inspection. Highlights include:

Cuffs; Vary a lot. Knitted cuffs are snug and comfortable but when wet take far longer to dry than the fleece they are complementing. In winter weather they can even freeze. Cuffs trimmed with Lycra/ nylon avoid this. Doubled over fleece cuffs/trims are practical, but less substantial.

Zips; Most are now identical, but some feature a windstop flap inside. Nearly all zip pullers are the flip-over variety allowing the zip-in facility for many waterproof jackets. Full length zips = jackets. Half length zips = over the head smocks. Jackets have the advantage of offering better temperature control. Pocket zips may sport handy cord, or ribbon, puller extensions.

Pockets; Patch pockets (nylon fabric stitched onto a fleece), are attractive but vunrable to wear. Pockets should also double up as hand warmers, i.e made from, or lined with, fleece. Some smocks feature straight-through pocket handwarmers. (Both joined in the middle). This can also be handy for rucksack hip belts which can travel through them, leaving access and use of your pockets still open.

Hems; See cuffs, but many simply feature a drawcord design. I prefer this functional feature, especially when elasticated cord is used, as it offers practical heat control.

Also, have a look at shoulder seams. Cheaper options use more, which can restrict movement. As many fleeces stretch only one way, have the manufacturers used the fabric running in the best direction on arms and across shoulders?

Finally, although for pure warmth (in the hills, etc) it does make sense to choose fleeces that are snug fitting. I still feel compelled to say that nothing looks worse than a snug, or "correctly", fitting fleece. As manufacturers are so keen to shout about fleece being fashionable, wear them in a vaguely fashionable way; with a nice drape, slightly oversized, loose and comfortable.

Care. Keep well away from strong heat, as they melt easily.

THERMALS. (Or comfort layers).

These details are in addition to those covered in the "layering" section (Base layer) and polypropylene" in the material section.

As mentioned earlier, thermals aren't simply concerned with keeping users warm in cold weather but with helping keep the wearer comfortable over many different climatic conditions, whether atmospheric or personal, by lifting and transporting away perspiration.

The list of alternatives to the original synthetic thermal polypropylene, (see page 89) for similar products, is now a large and constantly growing one. As a taster it would include: (For silk, see page 90)

Meraklon; An effective and popular use/form of polypropylene.

Thermax; Is a crimped, hollow-cored polyester, which creates extra space to trap extra air.

ICI's Tactelfibre; These polyamide multifibres give good all round use. A thicker fleecy version exists for particularly cold conditions.

Two-layer combinations with cotton; A two layer knitted combination of cotton and, e.g, tactel fibres. The inner side, (Tactel) wicks away moisture, where the outer side (cotton) due to its large fibre surface area encourages evaporation. Other variations of this cross with cotton exist.

50/50 mixes of **polyester and viscose;** Very comfortable, good

General Clothing

wicking, but pills and not as warm as some.

70% Rhovyl and 30% Modal; A fine performer but not as soft as others.

Polartec 100; An effective extremely comfortable polyester. An antibacterial and soil relief treatment make it hygienic.

Rhovyl plus; An effective chlorofibre and viscose mix.

Some materials rely upon the natural characteristics of their ingredients, while others, (increasingly the more popular) use permanent hydrophobic coatings. By chemically etching yarns with water-loving and water-hating treatments, the pulling (loving) absorption mixed with the pushing (hating) refusal to absorb moisture, effectively transport perspiration away from the source. One example is: **Polyester,** once treated with a moisture absorbing coating, combined with the internal polyester and its water hating attitude = moisture spreads quickly = dries quickly.

The main advantages most modern materials and fabrics enjoy is the increased efficiency of wicking, faster drying times, easier machine washing and, most thankfully, anti-odour improvements.

In addition to the materials selected, different manufacturers use them in different designs, cuts and styles. Often the right fit can determine which product is chosen. Lightweight, medium weight, long sleeve or short, extra-long scooped backs, high collars, zipped necks, diamond cut crotches, lady's sizings and flat linked seams (no rubbing), can all go to influence a decision.

TRAVEL CLOTHING.

The tag "travel clothing" is often used to describe specialized lightweight cotton clothing. Regularly appearing with their own undeniable style and guise (plenty of zips, studs and pockets) they are usually unmistakable and have seemingly become the unofficial uniform for many outdoor enthusiasts, on and off duty.

During the mid-seventies, Rohan (in Milton Keynes) started it off. They originated the concept (as we know it today) of truly lightweight, functional and practical cotton trousers. These set the precedent for other areas of the wardrobe, all involving the use of thin, tightly woven, cotton or cotton mixes. Such clothing was not (and still isn't) intended specifically for walkers, but the hill walking and camping fraternity quickly adopted them as their own.

The idea is, clothing that offers advantages and comfort over a large range of conditions, climates and environments. Taking a typical pair of such "cotton walking trousers", the advantages include; Windproofing, and Showerproofing, or rather fast drying. (Most need to be regularly reproofed with many of the suitable products available from outdoor shops). High breathability. Cool in hot weather. Very small packsize. Plenty of zipped pockets. (Especially convenient on shorts). They'll wash in a hand basin and dry within minutes, requiring little, if any, ironing. Quality brands are very hard-wearing (sometimes more abrasion-resistant than denim), contrary to their light and thin feel.

From trousers, breeches, shirts, shorts, jackets, scarfs, waistcoats to skirts, such benefits and general concept has inspired all areas of clothing. An army of, essentially, "sons of Rohan" manufacturers now offer a large array of styles and choice. There is often a large sphere of quality between designs, manufacture (seams), zips and materials, with cheaper cotton being among the most obvious. Recent years have seen the slow amalgamation of other types and choices of materials and fabrics to be combined with or grouped with traditional cotton clothing ranges. E.g, micro fabrics, waterproof/breathable fabrics, lightweight fleeces, insulations and thicker brushed cottons.

LEGS.

Leg wear is usually the most confusing area of clothing choice, holding the most perplexity for many walkers. "What should I wear on my legs?", is a common question, but one that assumes a definitive answer. With the onslaught of the modern manufacturing of specialised walking equipment people have forgotten that these are in addition to their normal clothes. There needn't necessarily be an answer. Again, it's all personal preference. (Remember traditional clothes; skirts, tweed trousers, shorts, tracksuits? See "Understanding more about clothing"

General Clothing

page 89)

Modern cotton trousers (see previous Travel clothing) are immensely popular, as they are practical, but people don't feel as daft as they might with traditional breech options. However, such trousers are often inadequate for colder climates and restrictive in movement, making alternatives necessary. You could wear thermals under such trousers, but avoid insulated trousers for reasons described in the "layering" section, and overlook lady's tights. (Nylon = discomfort).

Typical features often include; Polyester/cotton mixes. Nylon/cotton mixes. Double knees. Double seats. Zipped pockets, including unsightly side leg pockets. Some zips are made from individually moulded fibre glass teeth = stronger, reliable, lighter. Key's D ring. (For attaching keys). Side poppers, or zips, allowing easier access into top pockets.

Often such trousers are over-long, allowing you to turn them up to your own length. However, usually the material is so thin it's unsuitable for stitching, in which case, use iron up/stick webbing. Always wash trousers first, as many shrink in length on the first wash. Personally, I've found simply rolling them up (wearing them as turns ups) avoids many complications.

Every boy scout knows not to wear denim (jeans) as this absorbs masses of water, taking ages to dry (accelerating heat loss) and contracts when wet, making walking difficult.

On cooler days many people appreciate the free-feeling comfort of many fleece, jogging type, trousers available. There's a large choice, but for most occasions I would suggest the thinner variety. With such items, always pack windproof (or waterproof) over-trousers, in case any winds turns particularly cold and severe.

Increasing in popularity daily, although for most, still looking a little too radical, are stretch (but not tight) "tracksuit type" bottoms, of which a handful of options exist. (E.g, "Ron Hill Tracksters"). They offer comfort and great freedom of movement.

Breeches (or plus-fours) aren't as popular as they once were, but unquestionably are as practical as they ever were. It's a shame that people's vanity has overridden the performance of the design, especially the many excellent modern examples. Personally, in the classic of walking meccas (national parks, etc) I can't see anything wrong with the breeches look. In many parts of walking country you would almost look daft without them.

Worn with knee-length socks (stockings which can be rolled down to control temperature), modern breeches offer a splendidly comfortable performance. There are different materials for different seasons. (e.g. cotton = summer). The best type are of the stretch variety, as they are extremely comfortable, windproof, moisture-wicking, easily washable, extremely durable and fast drying. Try a good quality pair on and you'll be sold. The leg should reach below the knee. Wool, corduroy and moleskin (which isn't real skin, but cotton) are traditional options. Avoid knee closures using velcro. Nice details include: double seats, zipped pockets (with gussets for easy entry) double knees and non-nylon internal drop pocket linings.

GAITERS.

Usually wrap-around covers for the bottom of the legs, when the need for full waterproof trousers is insufficient. e.g, walking through long wet grass. They may also be used to stop rain running from over trousers inside boots. A reasonably universal design; a metal hook to attach to boot laces, with cord/laces tied under boot (however you wish) and a drawcord at the top to hold them up. (Short ankle height versions are called stop tous)

Some people find gaiters extremely useful, while others simply don't bother.

The better type are elasticated around the bottom hem and have full length zips positioned at the back of the leg. Different waterproof nylon weights are available; the lighter = more flexible, but less durable. Canvas (or cotton duck) versions offer durability and breathability. Relying on the cotton content swelling when wet, they are reasonably watertight. Best for; tough protection from heather, bracken, etc. They are improved with suitable proofing.

Waterproof and breathable versions do exist (e.g, Gore-tex. See

General Clothing

Waterproof chapter) but their relatively high cost often makes their use in this vunerable area questionable.

One particular brand of boots incorporates into the soles special groves and shapings designed to accommodate a specially tailor-made, near watertight, gaiter, covering the bottom leg and entire boot, leaving only the tread pattern exposed. (These products have many devoted users, but are generally best appreciated in snowy, winter conditions, as they can take a bit of getting on and off and have questionable wear resistance over rocks and scree).

SPORTS SANDALS. (For other footwear, see "Boots" chapter)

Unlike traditional sandals, sports sandals are, to most of us, a new animal altogether, offering new potential. An enormous success story in the States, being used for every occasion, they offer the British walker/camper genuine performance, support, comfort and (amphibious) potential for dozens of occasions when anything else is inadequate. At first they appear a very simple product and contradict their normal price tag, but once worn, it's easy to see how the cost relates to performance along with durability.

Put simply, they appear as a thick rubber slab with two velcro adjustable nylon (sometimes leather) straps over the foot and around the ankle. The sole offers a good support, (anti twist plus arch support), grip, shock absorption, control and fitting. They are as close to athletic sports shoes as sandals can get.

Originally (around the late seventies) the first sports sandals were crude and far too complicated (eight ladderlock adjustments), and never really took off to their full potential. In 1982 Teva spotted the space and introduced the first true designs, as we know them, remaining free from rivalry for years. Today there are a number of brands offering quality versions.

Most soles are made from EVA, often compression-moulded for shaped fittings. (Some brands use P.U and soft single density memory moulds). While featuring shock absorption, the sole should be firm enough to last, maintaining its thickness, especially offering no-roll comfort at the ball of the heel. Some soles come in moulded shapes featuring a lip running around the upper edge, protecting toes and feet from lipping over the edge and from stones. (But can hold water). Velcro webbing/strapping should be of the flat, but tubular, type as this avoids sharp edges digging in. (Some types include comfort linings). Avoid cheap imitations available in general high street and sports shops. Quality outdoor leisure shops will stock the genuine articles.

In the States there are special socks to increase use beyond the warmer months, but here, such sandals are still reserved for warmer seasonal use.

SOCKS.

These apparently mundane items hide an extremely competitive manufacturing market, but as a result provide us with many fine products. It was the outdoor walking-sock market that induced the change from sock sizing to foot sizing on socks across the entire retail spectrum.

No longer are traditional fisherman's socks readily available, but hosts of loop stitched varieties now rule the hills. Traditional rag socks (smooth traditional knit), are harder wearing, which makes them suitable for long distance walks, while loop-stitched socks (thousands of short loops on the inside) are more comfortable, but need to be washed most days and age quickly. But undoubtedly, loop-stitched socks do make for considerable improvement in comfort.

Double cylindrical knitting machines were invented by the start of the 20th century (used in earnest by the sixties) and enabled the production of loop-stitched socks. It takes such a machine only two minutes to knit an entire sock, with computers feeding it information of when to make a shape and add extra thickness. Once knitted, socks are then dyed, providing some pre-shrinking. Removed from the dyeing vats they are pulled over leg/foot formers (shapes) and left to "set". Heat treated, the sock's nylon content softens. Cooled off, the nylon resets, forming a neat presentable product.

When choosing socks, you should always wear what you get on best with, but most people wear two pairs for walking boots; a thin inner

General Clothing

pair and a thicker outer pair. The basic idea is that the inner pair and outer rub against each other (using up any friction). As discussed in thermals, for the very same reasons, the thin inner pair should also wick moisture effectively. (Blisters love dampness). There are many excellent polypropylene type options. (See polypropylene page 88). Avoid domestic nylon and cotton socks; at the very least, quality wool socks offer better performance.

Over these a typical loop stitched walking sock should be worn. These provide general cushioning and comfort. (Not ski socks. These have a poor fit over heels and usually contain too much nylon).

Most examples of quality socks will have a small nylon content. Not an economy feature but necessary to add extra durability and a comfortable stretch fit. (The wool should be colour dyefast to avoid staining boots or feet) They are available in differing lengths. Most opt for the mid-calf height, while people wearing breeches require knee length varieties. Fully loop-stitched up the entire leg offers extra warmth, while ribbed versions (patterned & thinner) are preferred for most occasions.

One feature often shouted about is the presence of a "flat linked toe seam". (This avoids uncomfortable rubbing over the top of toes). There are two main methods: firstly, you can create a smooth flat seam, but to the sacrifice of loop-stitching across the immediate area. This offers no insulation for toes in cold weather and little durability and resistance against wear. The better, second, version features a traditional seam, but trimmed down in bulk and squeezed, reducing its presence.

The Thorneburg Hosiery (USA) started the latest trend some years ago when they introduced their first high-tech socks. The most obvious difference was the addition of extra cushioning and protection against abrasion and blisters. The logic can also be reversed offering protective, but lighter, cooler, socks by eliminating bulk from all areas except the vital ones. Along with the sole use of synthetic, high wicking, fibres, which proved more durable than wool, eventually other features included; Spandex instep, (arch) providing support and lift. Flat knit side panels, improving ventilation and reducing compression.

Now, there are a small army of similar products, many arguably better than others. A large slice still favour the use of wool and believe that nothing has yet rivalled it in sock performance. (Totally synthetic socks can be difficult to dry overnight when saturated and offer no warmth once wet).

Some socks feature double cuffs (double thickness) and extra cushioning around the ankle. Some have Lycra ribbing around/over instep, holding socks in place. Others may use wool which has worsted spun yarns. (Bristly short fibres combed out, improving uniform quality).

CARE. Wash socks inside out. Don't bother darning holes, as this can easily cause sore spots. When camping for a few days try to, at least, rinse out with cold water. Using lining socks reduces the need to wash the outer pair, but if drying inners on camp, don't let them near direct heat. (The fibres can melt).

GREEN CLOTHING.

There exists an irony and dilemma for people who are active in the outdoors, as they are people who require performance clothing but who are traditionally regarded as, and usually are, environmentalists. We want the best clothing, but at what cost?

Manufacturers are aware of the contradiction but generally seem more concerned with promoting "fashion with function". What about "friendly?" Some manufacturers, have surrendered to green audits, which is a commendable action. Some manufacturing processes have achieved "clean" awards, including those of "W.L. Gore", "Malden Mills", who exceed required regulations and "AKZO" (Sympatex) who recycle their heat and water.

Cotton is traditionally considered to be an environmentally friendly material, as it is natural and biodegradable. However, cotton crops require large quantities of harmful pesticides. In the U.S.A such chemicals affect the soil and have been associated with land workers' illness. Unfortunately, green cotton, or organic cotton, (no use of chemicals) is of comparitively low quality. Besides this, as cotton engulfs 5% of the world's productive land, combined with its requirements for large amounts of water, it is seen as a major threat to water supplies. Once a large producer, but low on water, Israel no longer grows it.

General Clothing

On the other hand, nylon and polyester are petro-chemicals which are nonrenewable resources, although polyester is recyclable. (Often as plastic bottles). As many modern outdoor fabrics are made from polyester, why not recycle polyester for the manufacture of fabrics? As I write, the process has begun; Malden Mills (leading manufacturers of fleece) have started their own Post Consumer Recycled (PCR) fleece. Made from Trevira 2 (over 50% recycled polyester) it recycles, mainly, drinks bottles. AKZO (polyester laminates & fibres) have also begun practising PCR, helping to save on landfill space.

In Europe, Vaude now operate their non-profit making "Ecology" system. Garments made entirely from polyester (including zips, etc) can be returned to retailers, and then on to outdoor equipment manufacturers Vaude, for recycling. To produce recycled yarns requires a lot of polyester garments, but small quantities can go to produce zips and studs. I watch with interest, to see if this American trend lasts and spreads.

British manufacturer, Berghaus, were the first to turn their fleece off-cuttings into non-profit making, children's garments.

Gore (producers of Gore-tex fabric) are investigating if shredded fabric, mixed with soil, can provide a substance suitable for crop growth in areas of bad soil erosion.

In this industry, manufacturers certainly have a clean record of production methods, but paradoxically, nearly all are often producing products that could be greener.

Generally, the most effective way we can personally impose environmentally sound shopping is by choosing products that last, simply reducing, or slowing the problem.

SOME GENERAL POINTS.

For walks of any distance, duvet jackets (heavily insulated) have fallen in popularity, due partly to milder winters, but mainly because they are impractical for all the reasons covered in the "layering" section at the start of the chapter. Down duvets are still popular for camp-sites during the evening, particularly on trekking holidays and for use by mountaineers. (See the benefits of down in the Sleeping bags chapter, plus details for synthetic waddings). Waterproof duvets should have anti-wick strips around the inside hem.

Gone, from the modern minds, are words such as "Anorak" and "Cagoule", which are probably two of the most misused descriptions anyway. Judging by the wide variations of the opinion of just what "Anorak" is supposed to describe, it's now anyone's guess. Surprising to most ears, Anorak was originally a pull over the head, hip length, garment, while a Cagoule was a knee length version. Jacket is the simple and accurate description for these.

Fashion? Many manufacturers claim their products offer function with fashion. Don't believe them; it's myth. If you're middle aged, simply getting you to wear bright colours doesn't make you fashionable. Often quite the opposite. For many designers, I think the party is over. Instead of producing the usual practical and functional designs, then jazzed up a little, (i.e bright colour flashes on pockets, etc) manufacturers should now be in the position (with modern skills & knowledge) to design great looking garments, that are then provided with the practical advantages, reversing the current logic. Are such clothes fashionable simply because they tell us so? The Emperors clothes spring to mind.

The word is "breathable". Masses of consumers totally misunderstand what this means. Manufacturers are to blame. Throw in the word breathable on any type and area of clothing and it helps sales. When are we going to get breathable stoves? Anything with "breathable" on it, is a surplus word, simply pointing out that it isn't "non-breathable" in which it rarely has anything to do with improving breathability. (The only area in which it carries genuine weight is waterproofs, which are traditionally associated with clamminess) Epitomizing this misinterpretation is the occasional question, "Is this cotton shirt breathable?"

CARE.

One problem with many modern garments is the contradiction in care advice from many individual labels, which represent different

General Clothing

take into account the needs of separate materials, manufactured elsewhere. e.g, a jacket's waterproof shell and it's separate special insulation. Always follow the label of the manufacturer who produced the complete garment.

Store garments hung straight, cool, clean and dry. Dry garments in an airy place, away from direct sources of heat.

Clean: Follow manufacturer's instructions. Dry brush. Wash with soap flakes or Grainger's G-clean.

Reproofing: Graingers Fabsil = lightweight woven fabrics = polycottons and coated nylons.

Graingers Nylopruf = light (mono filament) nylon.

Grainger Superpruf = reproofs outer shell and water-shedding properties of breathable waterproofs.

(Graingers is available from outdoor shops)

MANUFACTURERS: The following is only a representative handful of quality clothing manufacturers. There are too many to mention, but a selection would include:

Rohan. Arguably still the best lightweight travel clothing manufacturer. (More mainstream than they once were). Excellent stretch breeches.

Other similar, top quality, names (making similar kit) include; Abris, Mounatin Equipment, Lowe Alpine, Jack Wolfskin.

Tenson make many beautiful and windproof cotton jackets.

Quality fleece garment manufacturers are abundant, but the better names would include; Berghaus, Karrimor, Sprayway, Mountain Equipment, Climbing 4, Lowe Alpine, Northface, etc, etc.

Craghopper, make quality, good value, stretch breeches.

Peter Storm, supply, amongst other things, proofed (waterproof) quality pure wool jumpers.

Lakeland, Burton McCall, Thorlo, Lowe Alpine, make socks.

SUPPLIERS OF THE FINEST DOWN CLOTHING AND
SLEEPING BAGS IN THE WORLD FOR OVER 33 YEARS

Full colour catalogue available:
MOUNTAIN EQUIPMENT
Dept. HK1, Dawson Street, Hyde, Cheshire, SK14 1RD

Photo: John Dunn, Cape Collinson

Mountain Equipment

SLEEPING BAGS

A key piece of equipment that transforms the walker to backpacker or camper, the sleeping bag makes braving the cooler temperatures of a night under the stars more attractive. Not only does it produce a warm personal environment to protect us from the chills of a sunless sky and frosting grounds but it also counterbalances the reduction in our own heat generation as we sleep, in one lightweight package. All this is no easy task and calls for knowledge and skills only really understood and achieved since the end of the seventies.

Once upon a time a thick blanket was all many a sleeper had to comfort him, just about keeping off the damp. After the war there were plenty of army surplus sleeping bags but these were heavy and hardly an improvement. By the seventies there were people in the business of manufacturing and supplying the growing outdoor fraternity with bags made specifically for the job, but again these, in retrospect, were barely an improvement on horse rugs and carried a hefty price tag. The problems weren't so much to do with the insulating materials, as down was at hand, but more with what to actually do with it. Utilising it properly and incorporating it into a bag that would make the best of what insulation it had, using various manufacturing techniques, were where improvements would lay and where faults could be eradicated.

The most obvious change all modern outdoor bags display is their overall mummy-type shape. These "mummy bags" are a vast improvement, for warmth to weight efficiency, over traditional rectangular bags . By tapering down, inwards towards your feet and hugging your overall shape they provide a warmer environment while using less materials and bulk. Unlike rectangular bags (used for caravanning, boats, etc) there are no empty areas to unnecessarily dissipate and lose warmth.

Most bags these days will look similiar but all fall into their own categories of warmth. With mummy sleeping bags this is generally accessed by the use of "season ratings". Unlike domestic duvets, it

111

would be misleading to attempt to allocate a tog type rating system, as unlike bedrooms, camping locations, conditions and environments can vary and all impose differing results upon a bag's performance. It's important to remember that all suggested season ratings are approximate, not only does one person's metabolism vary from the next, but manufacturer's optimisms also seem to vary. One brand may feel that a bag capable of reaching down to 5 degrees is a comfortable three season bag, while another may consider this a four! Even then, trying to establish what is comfortable opens up more room for imagination. I always say that any bag is capable of going down to -60 degrees, but just how warm you'll be is quite another matter!

One or two manufacturers are actually very realistic and have devised their own independent systems of fairly establishing a measurement of a bag's performance, but as these are few and far between we must use the knowledge within the following pages, letting season ratings serve only as a clue. How season ratings work is very simple. A four season bag would include suitable use for a British winter, while a three season bag is capable of use through spring, summer and autumn. A two season splits spring and autumn in half, adding the two warmer halves together and joining summer to make a total of two. Naturally a one season rating belongs to summer. Five season rating bags exist to accommodate anywhere in the world that serves up a much harsher winter than ours. These might also be referred to as expedition bags.

Why we have different warmths of bag is often puzzling for some people following the logic of: if a winter (four season) bag is warm enough for the coldest time of the year, then it should provide all year round performance. Why bother with, or choose, a three season bag? The simple answer is that a winter bag would be uncomfortably warm for summer use, while also making most of its extra weight totally unnecessary. An important point if, like all backpackers, you wish to keep all weights to a minimum. Even car boot campers should find the over warm performance annoying. True that with the aid of full length zips, the user can regulate the warmth, but this is an occasional necessity allowing fine tuning of even the most correctly selected bags.

Season ratings also highlight another area of sleeping bag ranges which probably cause the most confusion. Often a potential consumer will find a 4 season bag selling at considerably less than a nearby

Sleeping Bags

summer season bag. One bag that feels considerably loftier (thicker) than another may also cost substantially less. This all relates to varying qualities and constructions. One bag, with superior and wiser construction techniques, may achieve the same warmth value as a neighbouring bag while using considerably less insulation. (This will usually result in a lighter and smaller packing product). One down-filled bag using less down than another may easily provide the same warmth but cost more because of its better construction, also it achieves a lighter and smaller pack size.

There are many seemingly strange and contradictory sleeping bag scenarios, but a logical mind can quickly make sense of them.

The following pages will outline the varying qualities of material and construction which dictate weight to performance and price to value.

(Note: All sleeping bag's constructions are outer, insulation and inner).

INSULATION.

Insulations have to do two things, provide loft, to capture a thick air layer and secondly, stabilise it.

The first reason: The major cause of heat loss is conduction. Air is a very poor conductor and by weighing nothing becomes the obvious and best choice for insulation. But...

Secondly: It's understood that convection loses heat. This is when moving air carries away warm air. E.g, when a fan or breeze cools our skin. So to avoid this the best way to preserve warm air is to stabilise it. Simply by stopping it moving about as much as possible enables it to hang around longer. This is what an insulation's role is.

Concerned with warmth, all insulations must therefore capture a maximum layer of air, stabilising it efficiently while interfering with this, perfect non-conducting, air layer as little as possible. This is usually accomplished by achieving a large surface area of filling material with the minimum of weight.

All insulating materials fall into one of the two categories: Down or Synthetic.

DOWN.

For a long time the only real option, down now only really caters for and survives at the top end of the market. Arguably still the best material for the job available to Man today, it's warmth to weight ratio (the amount of loft it can achieve from so little mass) and ability to constantly be crushed down to a snip of it's lofted state, without damaging it's recovery performance, is amazing. In a phrase, light, small, durable and warm.

However, down does suffer some possible disadvantages, which by contrast, happen to be all the advantages of synthetic, as we'll discover later.

Basically the insulation from the breasts and undersides of ducks and geese, down has never been convincingly equalled, or not at least at the highest qualities and grades. Development of synthetics has improved all round performance so effectively that lower grade down bags have been made redundant. Down bags incidentally could only really improve once fibre technology had improved. Most lightweight nylons weren't down proof. Only the true top quality down sleeping bags (considerably dearer) can still argue a clear performance lead. Lower priced "down" bags can still be found with costs comparable with some of the dearer synthetics, but it's generally agreed that a genuine quality down bag should be expected to demand over twice the price of a competent synthetic.

Down is an umbrella word, as many different grades exist, usually referred to and described as "fill power". (Strength/retention of warmth and recovery rates). Rare these days, cubic inches are used in the measurement of fill power. This is when one ounce of down is left to expand inside a cylinder. The higher it lofts the better, often scoring around 550 to 650 cubic inches. (The different grades of down are sorted by the use of short blasts of air).

While it is said that larger waterfowl, i.e. mature geese, provide the best known examples, reaching a prime in early winter, good duck down can be considered better than a poor goose down. Most manufacturers use a blend of both anyway. Down described as "white" can only possibly argue some kind of hygienic improvement, or suggest associations with some winter birds.

Sleeping Bags

Ever since the seventies, China has been associated with the supply of around seventy percent of the world's down, while it has been noted by some that overall down quality across the world has dipped since its increase in popularity during the fifties. Towards the end of the seventies many foreign products were being stuffed by grades supplied even by tropical birds; a very poor standard, as creatures living in colder climates naturally produce thicker, stronger down.

Today some manufacturers of down bags use a chemically waterproofed down, but users can also proof their down bags (with no interruption to loft) with products available from outdoor shops. This can prove an advantage, as we'll discover later. Many manufacturers resist such treatment as they feel one of the main functions of down is to draw moisture away from the body, (down has good hygroscopic attributes = moisture absorption and discharge) with which some such finishings can interfere slightly.

Take heed of the phrase "new down" as some have been known to use "couchee", a recycled fill, salvaged from old down products.

The cheaper down bags naturally enough use the lower grades of down (less loft = heavier) but usually with the addition of feathers. A percentage of feathers, often around fifteen to twenty, is added purely and basically to keep down the overall cost. This unfortunately has the result of simply increasing the weight, while reducing the even distribution of insulation. (These percentage volumes can be misleading as they indicate a greater share of down than may be present. This is due to down being much lighter than feathers whilst having much greater filling capacity. The truer and more accurate description is found by using weight percentages. Soon this will be a legal requirement across Europe).

It seems that these bags only really exist to cater for the people who have decided they want a down bag and nothing else, whilst not entertaining the higher price tags. In fairness, due to the cost of the actual down along with the required labouring skills of using it to its required, potential, only down bags at the far higher end of the market justify consideration.

Important; At the risk of confusion, while down and feather mixes do occur as an economy drive by many, the majority of high quality manufacturers also employ the additional use of some small feathers as they believe pure down bags are too sensitive to pressure alone (losing loft) and stick together when damp.

SOME DOWN FACTS; It would take 15-30 birds-worth of down to fill a down jacket and around forty for an average sleeping bag. A good reason why down retains warmth is it's percentage of "keratin" (also found in human hairs and wool) which acts badly as a heat conductor. Only the air is lighter; down weighs just 1.0 - 4.0 mg. Unlike feathers, down has no quill, just a small core, from which its hairs disperse. It takes 400,000 to 1,000,000 pieces of down to make around one kilogram of filling.

SYNTHETICS.

The brief; to create man made down. The conclusion to date? Very nearly. Since the first simple polyester strands and weaves of the late forties, synthetic waddings (insulation) have evolved remarkably and now in many instances provide an even better alternative to down. Many manufacturers (chemical industries) now produce differing versions of man made insulation, all contributing to the bewildering array of trademarks and names. Du Pont, producers of Quallofil insulation, Niedhart and 3M are only three of the many examples.

Most starter bags will use an unbranded polyester fill; just about adequate but could be better. To help improve the warmth, while maintaining or reducing the weight, of polyesters, the most common solution is to produce hollow fibred polyester. The simple logic here is: Hollow = for the same amount, mass, or weight, surface area is increased, reducing and stabilising more air movement. More air stabilised, equals more warmth. This is most classically displayed with Du Pont's "Hollowfill". (An actual trademark, hollowfibre a description). Improving on this further, "Quallofill", also by Du Pont, enlists the use of several hollows, all within a single fibre. This maintains the volume of air retention, (some increase in thermal resistance by 20% over standard polyester), strengthens the structure and most importantly of all reduces its own weight further. They also pack down smaller, up to 16% of the original size.

Never becoming as common in sleeping bag use as some had once expected "Micro fibres" are a thinner layer type of synthetic insulation,

Sleeping Bags

(found more regularly in duvet jackets). The idea is that each fibre reduces air flow due to increased surface friction, which stabilises the air, rather than the traditional catchment of air in air pockets. Due to their tiny fibre size, many achieve up to twenty times more surface area, which equates to the increase of air friction (20% more). With hardly any loft, these waddings are relatively very thin, but offer nearly twice the warmth (per inch of thickness) of all competitors. Some examples absorb less than 1% of their own weight in water. So why aren't these new wonder fibres used more extensively ? Unfortunately sleeping bags require more than clothing, so costs come under scrutiny, but even in the higher markets are found lacking, sadly weighing up to forty percent more than equivalent down warmths. The final downfall is caused by their own density and stiff nature, resulting in very disappointing packsizes, along with the near exhaustion of their restuffing/packing.

In recent times the phrase "Micro fibres" has started to be used to describe similar but perhaps more mainstream insulations. The new loose use of the name is increasingly found describing cross-over type fibres. (An amalgamation of both types). Also commonly used to describe some very thin and fine fabrics. (See Clothing chapter).

To stabilise synthetic fibres, the most common method is to crimp them. This enables fibres to lock into one another. Twisting like a cork screw is another usual, but suspect, method. Slicing away at the fibre's sides, rather like peeling a banana, is becoming more popular as it impersonates down authentically. Many variations on similar themes exist in the world of synthetics; even careful blends and combinations of many different types produce better results and specific characteristics. Some use subtle blends of different materials and coatings all selected to provide unique qualities, rather like adding ingredients and flavours to soup. E.g, Some maintain their loft, after water immersion, far better than others. Some fibres will melt at a specific temperature and bond to others to improve strength. (Coatings are often silicone. This acts to reduce fibre friction and therefore increase loft. Quality fibres have this thermally applied, while cheaper brands are merely sprayed). But probably the most important common denominator for all fibres is the importance of volume to surface area. The higher the better.

THE MAIN PROS AND CONS OF SYNTHETIC vs DOWN.

Weight for weight, down is considerably warmer.

Weight for weight, down compacts far smaller than any synthetic. (= warmth for warmth, down is considerably lighter).

Synthetic is machine washable, while down needs to be hand washed. (With suitable down shampoo).

Synthetic dries quickly (useful if wet in the field), while down takes hours, possibly days.

Down needs to be dried thoroughly or it will rot.

Down is useless to sleep in if it gets wet or damp, while synthetics still retain up to eighty percent of their normal performance.

Quality down (the only type worth considering) is considerably dearer than synthetic.

A quality down bag can last over ten years.

Synthetics are moth-proof and non-allergenic.

Contrary to many down-devoted theories, synthetics often carry genuine advantages. In wet and humid conditions you would find it harder to spoil a synthetic's performance. A down bag would be harder to dry in damp tropical conditions, no matter how well you believe you can keep it dry. My general observation is that bearing in mind the considerably higher cost of down products even considering the product's longer life span, synthetics show excellent value for money and easily satisfy the vast majority of sleeping bag users today.

CONSTRUCTION.

A sleeping bag's construction is the true and all-deciding factor that determines good from bad bags. When sleeping bag specifications refer to construction, essentially they refer to how the bag's insulation has been utilised and stabilised. A sleeping bag's insulation is only as good as it's construction and a poor construction may need to use more insulation to achieve the same warmth. (Similarly a poorer insulating material may

Sleeping Bags

help to provide a warmer bag than usual due to intelligent construction). A bag's wadding needs to be stabilised in order to maintain an even distribution. e.g, avoid its bulk migrating to the foot region.

Concern about construction can generally be disregarded in dealing with starter and budget bags, while only minor or nonexistent alternatives exist anyway. It is realistically only with higher quality bags that we need to consider differences in internal details.

With down the strong necessity to discipline its movements, without reducing loft, is answered by the use of channels. By creating various compartments (baffles) the down's migration, and possible thickening and thinning, is restricted while lofting retains full freedom. It's this compartmenting that can absorb much of a down bag's cost while requiring genuine skills in the stuffing and even distribution of filling.

Most early down bags and a few modern summer season bags opt for the more obvious and far simpler method of segregation; one large down bag, stitched through. This is when the use of simple single lines of stitching join the outer shell and inner lining together, acting to block any shifting of down, at spaced intervals the full length of the bag. This is adequate for summer bags, but anything requiring extra warmth, without any extra bulk/weight penalty, needs to avoid the regular depressions and thinnings of insulation that this system unavoidably induces. (The outer and inner materials joining together crush and restrict the down at regular depressions resulting in areas of heat loss).

Due to the nature of down, we know that the best solution is to employ deep baffling or chambering, but exactly of what style and type? So many, only slight, variations seem to exist. Most manufacturers' brochures will provide you with many different basic cross section illustrations but usually all are much of a muchness. If you were to line up a row of bread loaves, with their long sides touching, observed from the sides, this is pretty much how most cross section baffles would appear. (Unusual in most down bags, some extreme versions may use double baffling. This is when an extra row is added on top. The centre of each new baffle overlaps the join, edge or sides of the first. This reduces heat loss through stitching).

Channel-sewn H-chambers, channel-sewn diagonal chambers, slant box, slant wall, slant tube, cross block baffles, side block baffles, radial

119

double box constructions and general differential cut baffles are just some expressions and names given to the many different, but similar, styles of baffling. The most commonly used and heard is "off set" baffling. This is when the compartments lean towards an angle, creating a cross section of diamond shapes. All carry the common goal of providing maximum loft with the minimum weight of panels used for the actual channelling of the down.

Most bags arrive in the form of eight upper and eight lower separate down chambers, but some have over four times this amount. Naturally the more the merrier, but the more the heavier! The better bags use baffles that run vertically over the chest region (rather than the traditional horizontal) as the natural curvature of a chest and shoulders may encourage down to fall either side of the extremely important chest region, leaving it poorly insulated. Vertical baffles at the chest avoid this.

Most sleeping bags reserve the majority of down for the top layer of the bag, as the lower side would only crush instantly under the user's weight. (The underside should be catered for by quality ground insulation. See chapter, Rollmats.) Some flexible down bags take advantage of down's nature and allow the deliberate shifting of the down's location. By allowing horizontal baffles to run, uninterrupted, the full length around and underneath the bag, the user is able to shake the down around to the underside. This freedom of redistribution allows the owners to dictate and select their own personal thermal requirements for varying climatic changes, whether seasonal or nightly. (This could be considered a coincidental advantage as it's also a cheaper method of construction).

Among the obvious legions of differing details, one design feature well worth mentioning is the use of elasticated thread. This subtle elastication on the inside of the bag (not on the outside as this would impede lofting), increases the bags snugness. (It is not restrictive). This in turn reduces air movement = more warmth. Reduced air being pumped out through the top, like a bellows = more warmth. Which ultimately means that less down is required = an even lighter bag!

Protection of the important extremities, foot designs and baffling around the base of down bags has varied regularly in recent times.

Sleeping Bags

While allowing feet to sit up straight (unlike trad-rectangular bags) complex solutions often emerged to solve the problems of migrating down around this small area. Recently though it seems that the simplest of designs has finally laid the arguments to rest. A "why didn't anyone think of it earlier?" type of solution; a simple large block of down is wedged into the bottom. Sitting in-between the upper and lower baffles this stop gap provides an effective and much cheaper answer. Compared to traditional multi-section designs it also saves on weight.

Faced with similar problems synthetic insulations, due to their nature, require different methods of construction.

Synthetics tend to arrive in sheet form of different thicknesses for different jobs. Simply stitching this within a sleeping bag is inadequate as the insulation would soon deteriorate and redistribute itself unevenly. To help reduce air movement inside the bag, synthetic insulation, along with down, also needs to be stabilised.

The cheapest and simplest solution is to stitch it into place, anchoring it to the outer shell. This is fine for many budget and summer bags, but is also the area that most shoppers armed with a whiff of sleeping bag knowledge get excited about, as for most cooler occasions it's limited in warmth. As discovered with down bags, rows of reckless stitching minimises the insulation's all important loft over most areas of the bag. This obviously would create cold spots.

The most common solution is to simply add a second identical layer, but with a staggered effect. The accompanying layer's rows of stitching start at the highest point of the loft on the bottom layer, creating an off-set effect. (Each layer is halved in thickness to maintain the original total thickness). This may be referred to as "Double off set" quilted or layered. Many slight variations exist on this theme, the most common is the use of a "loose outer shell". This is when the bag's outer plays no part and remains smooth, free from rows of stitching. This may slightly improve warmth.

Other alternative systems include; spiral formed chambers (similar to some shingle designs. Fibres don't lie flat and so create more loft), roof tile, or shingle design constructions (as the name suggests, layers of insulation seen from the side are similar to roof tiling, they create more pockets for more air to be trapped, while also lofting quickly) and laminated systems.

These laminated systems (or full loft constructions) are of note as they introduce an original improvement over traditional designs. Not trying to work out what to do with insulation, it backtracks further to the cause of stabilising synthetic insulation. No stitch-through constructions are necessary as the original layer of insulation has undergone a lamination treatment. Essentially a durable resin type finish is added. This make the material in its own right, strong enough to go it alone within the sleeping bag's inner and outer, secured only at the edges. This in turn means the bag's loft is never interrupted, equalling more warmth, so less is needed and so you can have either a lighter or warmer bag.

THE OUTER. (Shell)

Naturally outer materials should help maintain a lightweight finish, be flexible, silent (for sleeping), durable, damp resistant, have good tear strength (wet and dry), be compressible, and generally pleasant.

The answer is nylon. A straight forward taffeta nylon on budget bags or more deluxe versions on classier numbers. e.g, Rip-stop nylon. Seen closely this material shows s pattern of criss-crossing lines, or squares, which help strengthen a much lighter material. A much finer nylon weave is used (reduces weight) but to replace any lost strength, thicker stronger threads should check any mishaps.

Many sleeping bags employ the use of "Pertex" (a patented range of nylon materials, made in the north-east of England), whose general characteristics make it ideal for sleeping bags. There are various types used by many bag manufacturers which include; Pertex parachute silk, a rip-stop nylon actually used for parachutes; it's extremely light yet strong and provides a beautifully soft handle. (Thicker versions exist). All pertex fabrics are now treated with Teflon to provide increased water repellency.

A quick mention that some sleeping bags are available with waterproof/ breathable outers, (usually Gore-tex. See chapter - Waterproofs) but these are rare and unusual and possibly only necessary for extreme winter uses. (i.e the likes of Everest, etc.) Be warned, you need a second mortgage for such products, as they run into the hundreds of pounds.

Sleeping Bags

A more recent addition to sleeping bags from W.L Gore is "Dryloft" fabric. Costing much less, this laminate fabric helps protect insulation from external and internal moisture, while being windproof and highly breathable. This is intended to help bags retain better loft and warmth.

INNERS. (Lining)

Whilst keeping weight to a minimum, obviously one of the lining's main concern's is to be comfortable. Most budget bags use cotton (often cheap Indian cotton) or polycotton. (With polyester = more durability). A better version, also found on many top quality bags, is a mixture of polycotton and viscose, which provides the natural comfort of cotton but includes a faster drying and more durable element. This material caters to the whims of users insisting on only the likes of cotton against their skin, but unfortunately is bulkier and heavier than the many excellent modern nylon liners.

Not like sleeping in nylon bed sheets, these liners are a desirable feature. Although to the uninformed, the look puts many off, they are in fact very comfortable in use. They warm up quickly, don't cling (unlike cottons, particularly when turning over), don't mildew, dry quickly, are colour dye-fast, extremely durable, strong and most importantly of all are truly lightweight and pack down extremely small.

As mentioned in the "outers" section, "Pertex" is a very popular example of such linings. (When a version is used as a liner, it's unsiliconised). Virtually 4,000 filaments per sq.cm (ten times thinner than a human hair), its ultra fine structure enables it to transport moisture (dry quickly), be highly abrasion resistant yet hardly register on the weighing scales.

(Some bags, intended for army use have been known to use a reinforced inner foot section, for people who might need to sleep in their boots).

USUAL FEATURES OF MUMMY SLEEPING BAGS;

Zips. Once half length zips were available but today just about all bags feature a full length zip. Early bags often lacked a zip altogether, so that no warmth could be lost through this uninsulated region, (this is still available on a tiny minority of summer down bags), but the many disadvantages, associated with general convenience and comfort, have seen these basic designs die out.

Most zips are of a double ended variety, which enables the user to open up the bag from both ends. This is particularly handy for ventilation, or even perhaps sticking your feet out altogether. For this purpose, some quality manufacturers feature a reinforced flap or bellows (often Oxford nylon) which avoids the possibility of tearing the actual bag at the base of the zipper.

Most zips have an additional puller for use from the inside, while "self-repairing" zips are zippers that unsnag easily.

(Very unusual, some bags have zips that travel down the side and across the base of the foot. Others may have zips that travel across the main body, from hip to opposite shoulder. But this eliminates use as a quilt.

All bags should be available in left, or right, hand zip options. If you're right handed, opt for a left zip. This is easier as it means you unzip from the inside across your body and vice versa. This also provides the opportunity to zip a left and a right hand bag together, creating what's known as a twin bag).

To avoid the possible snagging of zips on the inner linings many manufacturers back the teeth with a stitched-in "anti-snag" tape. This goes some way to combating the problem (simply unzip using your finger behind the teeth) while another effective way of avoidance is the addition, in the bag's lining, of lines of stitching situated along both sides of the zip. (This leaves no surplus material to catch). Other solutions may be found as part of the zip baffle...

Baffles. To avoid the danger of quickly loosing warmth through the bag's main zip, it is imperative that your bag has a side (or zip) baffle. This is a long tube of insulation stitched inside along the zip's length to insulate this unprotected region. All bags now have these but there are differing qualities. (Occasionally you may find a double baffle. This is a small baffle on either side of the zip, inside the bag). A cheap way to make a baffle is to stitch the zip on the outside of the bag, leaving

Sleeping Bags

a couple of inches of the bag's side to hang down over the inside of the closed zip. This is fine but encroaches on the bag's overall width. An additional stitched-in version is generally better. (Although it shouldn't be stitched directly into the main quilting as this would create another cold spot)

As mentioned at the end of the "zips" section, zip baffles can alleviate the problems of snagging zips. Either by trimming the contacting side with stiffer, anti-snag, nylon, or sometimes incorporating lines of stitching.

Usual on most four season bags and increasingly more common on many three, or less, season rated counterparts is the inclusion of shoulder baffles, or neck collars. This is an additional protruding piece of insulation that travels around the shoulder region-important addition on many bags as it helps to eliminate the pumping of air (warmth) out through the top of the bag as you move. It also keeps cold air out. These baffles are drawcorded (sometimes elasticated) to provide adjustability.

Hoods. As most of us know, much of our warmth is lost through our head, so the inclusion of insulated hoods is now a feature of all mummy bags. The hoods are drawcorded, to loosen or tighten, according to requirements. The better versions are tailored (cowl hood), which rather than gathering a flat round shape around your head, caringly encompass and fit you. This is less disruptive to loft and provides comfortable warmth often without the need to tighten the drawcords.

A dearer manufacturing method, but more practical in use, is situating the drawcord and its toggle on the opposite side to the zip. This simplifies operations.

Foot piece. An important area of consideration to keep extremities warm. Unlike traditional rectangular bags your feet should be able to sit up straight. This is usually achieved with a box foot, while some economy methods are also found.

A functional design suitable for summer or budget bags is a "fish tail" foot. This is when the bag's end is stitched together, left side to the right,

125

(rather than top to bottom) creating an upright pointed finish, not too disimilar to a fish's tail fin.

A "box foot" is a tailored box finish, which allows feet to sit up straight while providing good baffling. These days the most commonly found is the "circle foot", which is very similar to a box foot but in a circle shape. Some manufacturers go to the extra expense of a true circle foot, while others may, often unnoticed, only provide more of an oval foot. (This is still described as a circle foot).

The stuff sacks. One of the main duties of a modern bag is to pack down small. All bags come with their own stuff sacks for space-saving transportation. Each manufacturer prefers their own styles (including thickness and strength of nylon fabric), the most common, a simple tube bag with top drawcord. Some have nicely tailored snow-type locks at the top (an extra closing flap with additional drawcord) while most opt for the simple flap of fabric, anchored with a few stitches, which tucks in under the tightening drawcord.

Increasingly more brands are including, (or replacing the stuff sack with) compression sacks. This is a stuff sack with four additional strips of webbing tape and buckles attached which enables the further reduction of the sleeping bag's packed size. (These can also be bought separately. Compression spiders are when the webbing straps are separate from the stuff bag and are not permanently attached).

"When you say, just stuff it in,

is there any particular

method of stuffing ?"

Sleeping Bags

OTHER GENERAL AND MINORITY FEATURES OF NOTE.

Some sleeping bags incorporate concealed pockets. Useful security when sleeping with valuables in some dubious areas of the world.

Fire retardant sleeping bags are available. This is usually achieved by treated outers and a layer of a fire barrier wadding (between shell and insulation) running the entire length and width of the bag. This may also increase the bag's overall warmth.

Hanging-loops at the end of the bag, are handy, as this simplifies hanging when in storage.

Liner ties, at the foot inside the bag, are for attaching sleeping bag liners to. They stop the liners from twisting inside.

Rare, but some manufactures still occasionally incorporate within some of their bags reflective metallised sheets or layers. This was once the apparent way forward, as it's logic of reflecting warmth with a thin lightweight sheet, appealed immensely, but unfortunately in practice hardly worked. (The noise also kept many users awake). Traditional insulation reduces the conduction of heat, while these reflective barriers reduce the radiation of heat, most of it being reflected. (Adding up to 10F). Problems with it breathing (even with holes) and limitations in comfort range have led to it's virtual extinction. (Poor breathability = in minus temperatures the bag may be warm, but in above-freezing conditions it can create a sauna).

Tapes, or cords, at the top of bags are used to tie the bag over shoulders and enable the user to sit up, taking the bag with them.

On some down bags opportunities for refilling and replacing the insulation are provided. A series of zips and velcro closures open direct access to each chamber.

Removable pillow sections may reduce the need to wash the compete bag so often.

Internal foot sacks (on down bags) add extra insulation for people who suffer from particularly cold feet.

Some manufacturers display a "Quality Down" tag which indicates they are part of the "Study Group of Quality Down"; an attempt by some to standardize down qualities. Extra segments to zip into bag zips, increase the width of some bags.

GENERAL POINTS OF NOTE.

Beware- weights in brochures and on bags may refer to insulation weight and not total weight. (Fill weight sometimes refers only to the weight of one square metre).

The shape of mummy bags varies from one manufacturer to the next. Some are more generous and pronounced across shoulders than others. Because the nylons used are only available in certain widths, some manufacturers, to maintain good shoulder widths, have to make their bags in two layers. This means a seam has to appear down the opposite side to the zip, rather than simply doubling over a sheet of nylon providing top and bottom. Oddly, some cheap budget bags seem to copy this design, but for no apparent reason.

While it is common sense to wear warm clothes inside a bag, (it's a myth that nudity is warmest, at least when by yourself) it's actually not as effective as people have assumed. More warmth is effectively added with extra liners. Fibre pile liners are effective but pack down as large as sleeping bags. Thin materials, as used for thermal underwear, are smaller, though not lighter, help a fraction, but are disappointing. (Their logic works best next to active bodies) Thin fleece liners appear to be the best solution as they are quite small, lightweight and effective.

Silk liners can help, but are best regarded as small packing hygienic inners. The idea is you wash a liner instead of the bag. Cotton liners (mummy shaped tapered versions are available) can be warm in the winter, cool in the summer, but aren't light, really need to be aired and aren't quick drying. Pertex liners provide good carefree alternatives to silk.

Some American and Canadian manufacturers still create strange designs (square hoods, central zipping hoods, square bags, etc) but for practical reasons they are best left alone.

CARE.

Important with synthetic sleeping bags, never bother rolling up the bag to pack it away, just stuff it in its bag. (Start with the foot). This actually does the bag more good as the fibres aren't being compressed in the same direction each time.

You shouldn't leave bags stuffed up for long periods of time. When not in use, ideally hang bags in dry places. Or at least store it loosely.

Always air the bag after use. While the bag may feel dry, your body has given off nearly a third of a litre of moisture during the night. If bags are packed away damp (particularly down, and cotton liners) it may damage them irreversibly. When in the field you should, when ever possible, air the bags. Even a few minutes in the morning sun can improve its performance later that night.

On synthetics follow washing instructions. They are machine washable. Use only mild soap powder. Give extra rinses. Only tumble dry at a maximum of 40c or better still, drip dry.

Down requires more care. Hand-wash down in lukewarm water, using one of the many down shampoos available from outdoor shops. Many require long soakings (see instructions). As wet down can become very heavy, don't lift the bag straight out of the bath, as this may cause inner baffles to tear, but let the water drain away first. Rinse out the shampoo thoroughly several times, but don't wring, gently press out the excess moisture. Use a towel to absorb surface moisture. At this stage you can give the bag a spin dry. To complete the essential total drying, hang the bag vertically. As it dries give it occasional soft shakes to loft the down slightly. Eventually turn the bag inside out to finalize the drying. Down can be very stubborn about drying, so you must persist, even if the bag feels dry to the touch.

The use of sleeping bag liners can increase the life of the bag as washing is reduced.

If snow holing (or in contact with snow) be careful to brush any snow (no matter how light and dry) off before you sleep, as any rise in temperature will cause it to melt and saturate.

QUICK REFRESHER OF BUYING POINTS.

Starter budget bags are often perfectly adequate for users not intending to carry them, as their pack sizes and weight are irrelevant.

If you're going to get a down bag, get a decent one.

Good down bags are lighter and smaller packing, but synthetics are cheaper, faster drying and easy to care for.

Warmer, bags should have some form of off-set quilting.

Choose bags with a full length zip; double ended. (Are they anti-snag?)

All zips should be backed by a good baffle.

Modern nylon type liners are comfortable.

All bags have hoods, but the better ones are tailored. Avoid bags with flat feet. Ensure they are tailored. (e.g, box foot).

Are synthetic fibres branded, or at least hollow fibre?

Especially on winter bags, a shoulder baffle is a good idea.

Do the stuff-sacks come with compression straps?

See the bag packed up, and feel its weight.

Most shops will allow you (without shoes) to climb inside. (Check for shoulder width).

MANUFACTURERS. The following is only a brief selection of some of the better brand names and manufacturers to look out for:

Mountain Equipment; A British manufacturer of some of the world's best down bags. Also having a small, but excellent range of synthetic bags, M.E now produce bags of the highest quality but often at refreshingly good value prices. A standard hard to beat.

Sleeping Bags

Rab; also a popular quality range of British made and world class down bags.

Other quality down bag manufacturers include; Vaude, Big pac, Jack Wolfskin, Northface.

Vango; producers of many bags offering standards of quality and features not often found at such relatively affordable prices.

Snug Pak; (Made in Yorkshire by "Brett Harris") These are an extremely popular and successful range of synthetic bags offering many different levels of performance and price. Perhaps best known for a range of particularly small-packing synthetic bags. (Perhaps the smallest around). Also make fire retardant bags.

Ajungilak; with over a hundred years experience, this Norwegian (but with a manufacturing base at Milton Keynes) company make some of the finest bags around. Their quality of manufacture is particularly impressive. They are the only manufacturer to have on-site carding plants.

Buffalo; are British manufacturers of pile bags. A minority of users favour these designs as they are hardwearing, relatively inexpensive, durable, and, most of all, warm when wet. Buffalo use pile (a synthetic fluffy type material. See "Fleece" in "Clothing" chapter) in conjunction with Pertex covers, making them windproof and giving them good water repellent properties.

THE FOAM FIRM

All Beacons leisure mats are manufactured using top quality closed cell polyethylene foam giving good heat retention, water resistance and durability.

BEACONS PRODUCTS LIMITED

EFI Industrial Estate, Brecon Road, Merthyr Tydfil,
Mid Glamorgan CF47 8RB.
Tel: 0685 350011 (5 Lines)
Fax: 0685 388396

ROLL MATS.

Your Sleeping Bag is only as good as your Roll Mat.

A roll mat (or insulation mat) is the layer of protection that protects you and your sleeping bag from damp, frost and cold. No matter how good your sleeping bag might be, if you don't have any form of insulation underneath it, you're unlikely to appreciate its design, insulation and cost.

As it's the insulation inside the bag that lofts up, trapping as much warm air as possible, its effect is therefore minimal when its insulation is crushed. This is exactly what happens to the lower half of a bag when you lie in it. To replace this lost protection, you need to use some form of firmer insulation that can resist your weight and maintain the layer of air between you and the ground. The most effective, or common, solution to this problem has been a layer of close cell foam.

Ever since the first foam mats, introduced to Europe in 1966, the main solution has remained the same. (Introduced by Karrimor, hence the product and generic name often used, "Karrimat")

You may have seen these mats rolled up and strapped to the underside of rucksacks. They come in various widths and lengths but usually large enough to protect the main nucleus of the body, although, if you suffer from cold feet, it may be a good idea to opt for a six foot version.

The most obvious point you may observe when viewing a range of roll mats is the fluctuation of prices. This is mainly due to the only major detail to consider when choosing a mat; there are two different methods of production, creating two different levels of quality and performance. The cheaper, having been chemically blown, to create the billions of tiny separate bubbles; and the superior having been physically (or pressure) blown. All are made from polyethylene, while E.V.A is often added to physically blown mats to keep the foam flexible and soft while sustaining insulation and durability.

The two basic methods...

Chemically blown = chemically cross linked bubbles = large bubbles = extremely lightweight, but not durable.

Physically blown = physically cross linked bubbles = very small bubbles = improved insulation as each bubble contains less air and absorbs less body heat. Micro sized bubbles = durability vastly improved.

While the first method produces a perfectly satisfactory standard for most summer uses, the latter offers a much more durable equivalent, often lasting for the owner's entire camping career. With some poor chemically blown models a strong thumb and forefinger can often feel the bubbles bursting between them, while a nick or tear will quickly grow and end its usable life. But considering the costs of chemically blown mats they do offer good value for money, perfectly adequate for most occasional summer campers. However, sometimes for just over twice the price a physically blown mat, with its much longer life, provides for the more dedicated camper much greater value for money. (Most physically blown mats will withstand virtually any conditions).

The labels will always describe which of the two they might be, but a close inspection and squeeze quickly confirms which is the physically blown version, as its firmness regains its shape much quicker. Various manufacturers offer differing sizes, finishes and weights. Some are simply cut off a roll, others are made to size with rounded corners. Some have their own tie-up straps, while others feature two different densities sandwiched together. More recent evolutions produce mats moulded with series of ridges designed to reduce weight but still trap extra air. All of these options fall simply into the personal preferences category, but the most common and satisfactory thickness for a physically blown mat is approximately nine to ten millimetres, providing enough insulation for four season use in the U.K and most of the world.

If there's one thing that can be criticized about close cell mats, it is that they are unable to be folded neatly and tucked away inside a

Roll Mats

rucksack, as this would damage the loft and thickness along the fold, creating cold spots. (Although one designed for this does exist). Carrying the mats rolled up, strapped to the outside of a sack, or wrapped internally around the rucksack's walls, is a perfectly satisfactory system, but many people find this an inconvenience or simply cumbersome and unattractive. A more recent concept of insulating mats has, coincidentally, overcome this problem.

Self-inflating mats, designed for the same job, have become a common and popular alternative, usually preying on people's belief that a mat with air in must, like an inflatable mattress, offer much greater comfort. While it is true that close cell mats provide a little extra comfort and are designed purely to offer protection against the elements, it is still debatable whether these thin inflatables offer much more. Many people find that even this slight improvement makes their purchase necessary and are grateful for small mercies.

As the mats contain only soft foam they are able to be folded into a neat and small package, and why the mats are able to self-inflate. It works on a system of suction. When the mat is tightly rolled away, expelling all air, the soft foam inside the air-tight mat is crushed and reduced in bulk to achieve a good pack size. The open/close valve is then closed, avoiding any air being sucked and drawn back into the mat by the foam trying to re-expand. This is exactly how the mat re-inflates itself once the valve has been reopened. Only a couple of human breaths might be needed to finish the job. The valve is then closed.

The system works well, but potential purchasers should bear in mind that most are in fact heavier than their close cell equivalent, all are considerably more expensive, often four or five times so, and people might consider the logic of camping with such a vital piece of kit which always carries the possibilities of a puncture. (Different weights of such products are available).

Once again, these mats come in varying sizes, thicknesses and materials. The original, least costly and probably most common surface finish is a hard wearing, proofed air-tight, nylon. But growing in popularity are the new thin rubbery, skin mats, made from a P.V.C. They manage to reduce the weight, slim slightly the pack size, offer better protection against thorns and sharp stones, but perhaps most attractively increase the friction and grip on a sleeping bag. A problem with the nylon strain is that when a nylon shelled sleeping bag lies over it, the sleeper regularly finds himself sliding off it. (Although temporary sprays are available to help solve this problem).

MANUFACTURERS. Brands include...

Foam mats.

Beacons Leisure: Large, good value, range of mats. Many sizes and qualities.

Karrimats: The original Karrimat. Still a popular choice of styles, often including tie up webbing straps.

Inflatables.

Therm a rest: The original. Popular selection of sizes and thicknesses. (Now include non-slip surfaces

Artiach: Competitive quality range, including skin mats.

CARE.

With close cell foam mats, simply clean with warm water and store dry, away from strong sunlight.

With self inflating mattresses; Store unrolled, with valve open, in a dry place. In extremely cold temperatures, mattresses will take longer to inflate. Body heat will improve matters - Pack mattresses inside sack, closest to your body. Resist folding horizontally. Ideally, fold length ways once, then roll towards valve. With some skin mats, roll out air - close valve - fold length ways - reopen valve and roll up. Close valve.

To clean; inflate and close valve. Use a soft brush and mild detergent. Rinse and dry thoroughly before storage.

Avoid strong sunlight and insect repellen Suitable puncture repair kits are available from camping shops, and follow the general method or repairing bicycle inner tubes.

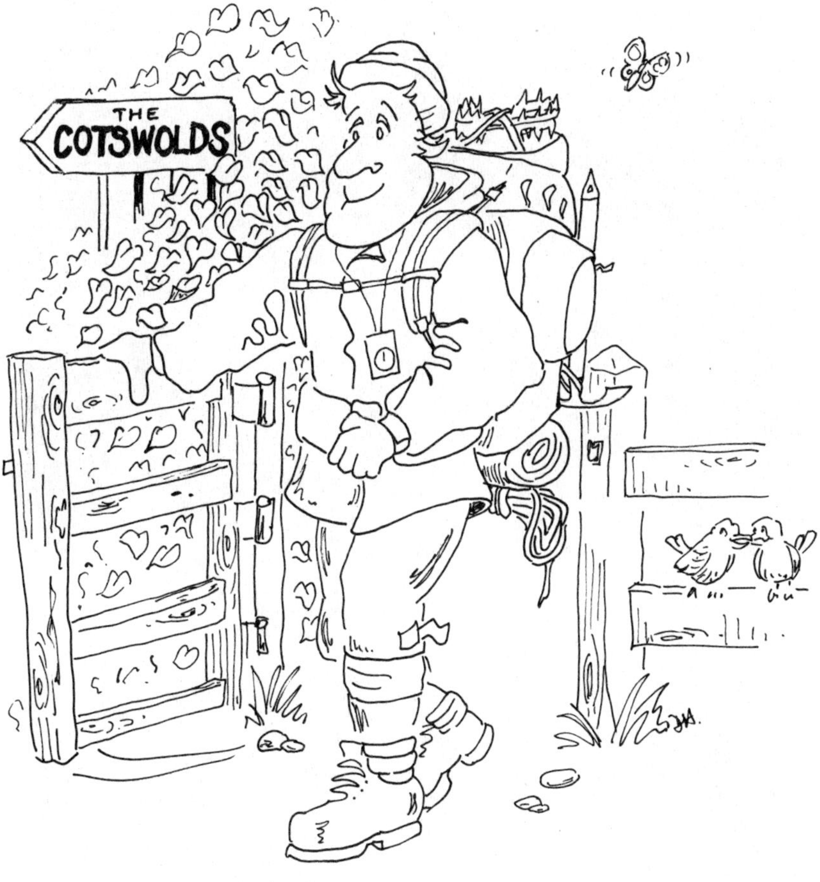
THE
COTSWOLDS

OUR LIGHT WEIGHT CARTRIDGE HELPS YOU CONQUER EVEN THE HEAVIEST GOING

Bleuet 470HP Stove

Bleuet 270M Stove

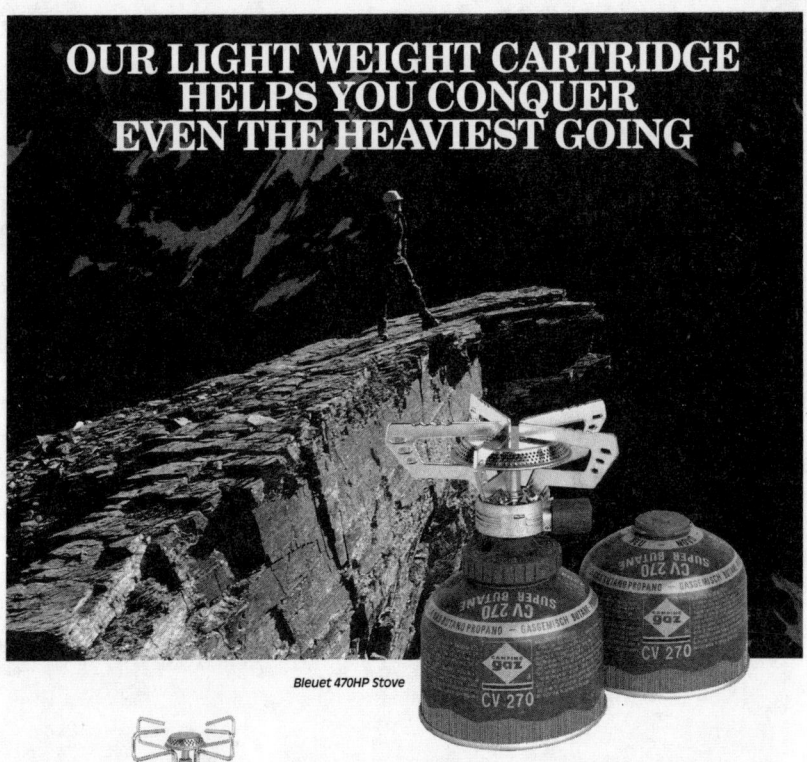

Whether you're backpacking in the Pyrenees or the Pennines you can't afford to carry any excess weight, that is why we've developed a system of compact valved cartridges, stoves and lights.

Our CV270 cartridge features our unique non-threaded, clip-on valve system which is safe and so simple to use, that even the coldest fingers can assemble a stove or light in seconds.

The CV270 is not only compact, but its low profile makes it superbly stable, easy to pack and combined with the powerful pocket sized Bleuet 470HP stove, you've the perfect travelling companions.

Just one CV270 cartridge gives you a whole 2½ hours cooking time and connected to the 80 watt Lumogaz 470 light, will illuminate your way for an incredible 6 hours. You also have the assurance that the cartridges' butane/propane mixture will perform well in cold conditions.

You can already find the CV270 cartridge in more than 20 countries including most of Europe, with the larger CV470 in 50 countries world wide, so however hard the going you're sure not to run out of gas.

Carena C Base Camp Stove on CV470 Cartridge

Lumogaz 470 Portable Light

Which all means that a little help from 'Camping Gaz' helps you go a very long way.

For further information on our range of stoves and lights, write for our 'Leisuretime' catalogue:

**Camping Gaz (GB) Ltd,
9 Albert Street, Slough,
SL1 2BH.**

CAMPING gaz®

'Camping Gaz'. Broadens your horizons.

STOVES.

An important tool for the camper, backpacker and even walker with a mid-day brew in mind, stoves provide convenient methods of food/drink preparation. Amongst equipment shopping lists, stoves offer considerably less choice, which for many is a blessing. Their simple designs offer relatively endless service, with choice of fuel creating the only major consideration. Often a case of weighing up the many pros and cons relating to what you require, but obviously stoves should also be light and compact. We'll discover other considerations as we go...

ALCOHOL STOVES. (i.e, Methylated spirit)

A simple burner wicks fuel up to jet holes. Simply ignite. No priming, no pressurising.

Forever popular, with the basic design now many decades old, the simplicity of these units carries many advantages. Using the most popular brand as an example, (Trangia; originally designed by John E Jonsson in the early forties) the main advantage they carry is the inclusion of all cooking equipment. (Two pans, fry pan or simmer lid, and sometimes a kettle, which boils water quicker). So while the complete package, at first, appears larger than other backpacking stoves, because the additional equipment tessellates down inside, (including wind shield), the true result is often far more compact.

Often portrayed as slow water boilers, such criticisms fail to appreciate overall time consumed setting up, filling, etc, and along with their efficiency in windy conditions, they are often, in real terms, the quickest.

Advantages: The only liquid fuel burnt unpressurized = safer. Not petroleum related = if split, it's clean and evaporates quickly. Trangias enjoy windy conditions. Unpressurised fuel means simple design = no faults, easy to repair/replace parts, next to no maintenance. Silent. Don't flare = safer for tent (doorway) use. Large base = stable.

Disadvantages: Amount of fuel required for a week's use = heavier than some alternatives. Half the heat of kerosene/etc.

Notes: Don't refill while burning. Invisible flame during strong sunlight. Many different names for meths around the world, e.g, Denatured alcohol, Marine stove fuel, Rod spirit. In Scotland you'll need to sign the poisons register. Dilute meths with 10% water to reduce soot on pans.

Notes on brands: Trangia models are available in two sizes; small = two/three man. Basic mini-Trangias (solo use) are now available. Teflon/non-stick coated pans, etc, are available singly or as a complete set but are heavier and require wooden cooking tools. On the other hand, pre-greased pans eliminate the need to carry cooking fats and think of the easy cleaning of last night's dried baked beans! Stainless steel pans are also available, tougher but far heavier, they may eliminate fears of illness associated with long term use of aluminium. There are now kits, available from either Camping Gaz, or Epigas, allowing the conversion to gas use. (Self sealing canisters. To follow) Trangias can be converted to Kerosene use, but this is very dear.

Optimus trapper meth burners provide improved heat control with a lever-operated air damper, larger fuel reservoir and a "safe fill" device.

PETROL STOVES.

They burn vaporised fuel. Heat from flames heats the main fuel line = fuel expands and turns to gas.

Recommended not to actually use with petrol/car fuel*, but with refined stove fuels. Ideally, use white gas (i.e, Coleman fuel) = pure naphtha = petrol with the usual additives removed = far longer gunge-free stove performance.

(*If you must, use low octane leaded (2 star) or with some stoves, unleaded.)

Traditional stoves that wick fuel up through the fuel line have to be pre-heated (or primed)* before igniting as the fuel won't have vaporise yet. Stoves with pressurising pumps are quicker and easier to light. (Except in extreme cold. Flames should be blue. Yellow = insufficient pressure)

Stoves

(*usually with burning paste)

Multi fuel versions are somewhat of a misnomer. (Fuel lines pass directly through flames) They still only run on stove fuel or white gas (virtually the same thing) or can be converted to paraffin use. (Which can be complicated).

Advantages: Efficient. Very hot. Fuel is widely available. It's also cheap, although actual "stove fuel" isn't.

Disadvantages: Longer to start up. Hard to light in the cold. Jets and tubes clog up = regular maintenance. Highly flammable = extra care. Can only refill cool stoves. Can flare.

Notes in general:

Refill in the morning, as you can only refill cool stoves. Wind shields vastly improve performance and efficiency. Don't totally fill fuel tanks as fuel may expand, reducing your pressurising of the stove.

Many have adjustable legs for uneven ground.

Such stoves are available in convenient (easier to pack) metal boxes, but are more difficult to pressurise.

Most stoves incorporate fuel tankers. One or two attach to special fuel bottles and pump units, which avoids over-heating fuel, makes additional fuel bottles unnecessary, deletes the need to refill stoves and usually provides a lower profile (more stable) design.

Burners used:

Roarer: Vaporised fuel jets out, ignites and bounces off a burner plate, splaying flames into a ring = noisy.

Ported: Flames appear from individual jets = improved control. Better for simmering.

Manufacturers include:

Coleman. Also make multi-fuel stoves and designs using separate fuel/pump units.

MSR. Produce stoves that will run on Coleman fuel/white gas, leaded petrol, unleaded petrol, paraffin, diesel and aviation fuel.

Optimus. Many popular options, including boxed designs. Also produce the Sigg fire-jet stove which operates off paraffin, Coleman fuel/white gasoline and unleaded or leaded petrol without the need to change the jet or generating tube and is impossible to over pressurise.

GAS.

Pre-pressurised gas cartridges (liquid petroleum gas) feed a jet which allows it to burn safely, with a valve for control. All use ported burners. (See last page)

Highly popular. Many models and choices exist. (Including size of gas cartridges available). Increasingly, ultra compact versions are produced, such as the Camping Gaz Bleuet 270M stove.

Cartridges/cylinders usually use butane gas, but this vaporises poorly near freezing temperatures. (Except at high altitudes. Thinner air = reduced external pressure = reduced resistance of gas flow). For cold weather, butane/propane gas mixes are easily available (usually 85% butane), as propane vaporises better in cold. The butane calms propane's volatile nature and allows cartridge weights to stay to a minimum.

Advantages: Clean. Simple. Excellent heat control. Relative low maintenance. Ideal for day walker users.

Disadvantages: As cartridges empty, performance reduces. You must carry empty cartridges until they can be responsibly disposed.

Notes in general: Alpine style stoves employ the use of a longer, flexible, fuel line, which attaches to gas from a distance = impossible to overheat cartridges, which can be very dangerous. They often include a "pre-heater" = the fuel line runs close to the flames, improving performance in cold weather. They are also usually more stable.

Look for stoves with anti-flare devices. (In case stoves are knocked over).

There are many "self sealing" cartridges now available. They are

Stoves

much better for the backpacker as cartridges can be removed and replaced before they are totally empty. (A problem with standard forms which are irreversibly pierced and quickly sealed by the stove).

Camping Gaz's CV270 "backpacker's" valved cartridges feature non-threaded valves, which can avoid the risk of cross threading or over-tightening. (Used with a 270M stove, on maximum setting, it will burn for three hours. Over seven hours simmering).

Self sealing and removable cartridges make transportation safer and allow stoves to dismantle and pack down smaller. Many such stoves also allow the convenient use of different sized cartridges; handy for adapting from day to week use.

Not generally recommended, in case of failure, but some gas stoves are available with electronic ignition.

Manufacturers include:

Camping Gaz: Many excellent designs. General refills are the most commonly available around the world, with their classic C206 cylinder available from over 115 countries, while the re-sealing butane/propane CV270 cartridges are now available from over twenty countries including all Europe. For group use, the Carena C stove is notable as it can provide 2,800 watts (boiling a litre of water in under 5 minutes) and operates off either the CV270 or identical, but twice as large, CV470 cartridge, from which it can operate for well over two hours.

Epigas: Inventors of self-sealing cartridges; there are many popular models using the system as standard. Are often compatible with other brand cartridges.

Others...

Paraffin (or Kerosene) stoves: Popular with many, these traditional stoves require priming fuels (e.g, meths, solid fuel), flare when igniting, take a fair while to get going and use fuel that stains badly and smells, but the units do last!

Solid fuel: Simple pocket-sized fold out stands allow the easy use of solid fuel tablets or jellied fuel. Hard to control, rather impractical for serious use, they are often seen as disposable items.

Dungburners: Unusual, and mainly found in America, a C-sized battery powers a fan, which flames a small fire, within a small metal stove. Fuel for the fire? Anything that will burn found around the camp-site. (Yes, including dung). Only a handful of models exist; their advantages are obvious. but so are the disadvantages. We'll have to wait and see if they catch on.

NOTE: Fuel availability. A major consideration for international travellers is local availability of specific fuels. Generally speaking there is usually one leading or most easily obtainable fuel. For example: Africa/Asia = Kerosene. Scandinavia = Alcohol (Meths). Alps/Pyrenees = Butane. North America = White gas (Coleman fuel).

CARE.

Danger. Read and study all instructions! Especially lighting procedures.

Avoid overheating gas cartridges and fuel tanks. (This includes heat rebounding from wind shields and wind sheltering rocks). Shield gas cartridges from strong sunlight exceeding 50 degree Celsius temperature.

Always ventilate if forced to use in a closed tent, to avoid carbon monoxide poisoning. Leave stoves outside the tent in case of fume leakage.

Carry fuels in suitable, made for the job, aluminium bottles. Don't fill to the brim, (strong sunlight/heat expands fuel) or leave for extremely long periods of storage. (Can corrode small holes).

Check rubber seals. (Especially on gas stoves with unremovable cartridges). Replacements cost pennies.

With alcohol and petrol stoves you'll occasionally need to prick open jet holes with wire prickers. (Pack some for long trips). Some petrol stoves feature built-in cleaning needles.

With some petrol stoves (relying on wicks) don't let the fuel run dry while in full swing, as this can scorch the wick, resulting in poorer performance.

Lichfield

A WORLD OF TENTS
WHATEVER YOU DO

WHEREVER YOU GO

WE HAVE A TENT FOR YOU

FOR DETAILS OF OUR FULL RANGE OF TENTS CALL OUR CUSTOMER
INFORMATION LINE FOR YOUR FREE COLOUR BROCHURE
OR WRITE TO:

John James Hawley (Speciality Works) Ltd.
Lichfield Road, Walsall, West Midlands, WS4 2HX, England.
Telephone: (0922) 25641 Fax: (0922) 720163

TENTS.

Many tent users, with or without childhood memories of nights under canvas, choose to do it, quite simply, because it's fun. Or at the least a desirable, enjoyable experience that seems to answer innate primitive calls. For the rest, sleeping in tents may simply be a means to an end. But no matter how much you curse the lack of a real chair, the boots that won't dry and the first awakening sounds of heavy rain, tents have come a considerable way in improving our comfort, energy levels and tolerance of nature's worst since the first of the wooden framed and canvas constructions.

A tent is an outdoor shelter which can be packed up, transported and reused, and the basic design spans many centuries. The hooped coverings of early narrow boats is one example of an historical design resembling many modern "hi-tec" tunnel tent designs of today.

After the original popularity boom for expeditions to the Himalayas and the need for tents that could allow the cost-saving transportation by mountaineers, and not porters, the first lightweight tents began to form. By the mid sixties still the only lightweight fabric alternative to cotton/canvas was a rather stiff polyurethane coated nylon, and that only offered next to non-existent waterproof standards.

By this time the traditional and standardised tent design was considered a great improvement if it featured "A" frames; two uprights joining at the top, greatly increasing strength over traditional single upright pole designs.

By 1970, Don Williams had modified his "Williams box" tent design, adding enough strength necessary for the first ascent of the Annapurna South face and perhaps unwittingly became the forerunner to the thousands of other alloy framed tents that would follow.

Soon, nylon tent fabric technology would improve, bringing along higher waterproofing levels, but also introducing problems with condensation, as, unlike cotton, proofed nylon didn't breathe- and so double skin tents were born. (Tents with inners and outer). Originally, many a confused camper considered their neighbours to be sleeping inside two tents. This new system also introduced sewn-in ground sheets as standard. Riding the crest of the new camping mad enthusiasm of the seventies, double skinned, alloy framed, nylon tents quickly demoted the traditional, faithful, and now old fashioned army type tents to Boy Scout troop duties; many, being over fifty years old, are still in active service.

This chapter deals with the tents of interest to modern backpackers and the like and does not include the usually basic and straightforward, family sized frame tents.

The modern day camp-site is adorned with dozens of differing traditional, and not so traditional tents, often bizarre, but all can be generally categorised...

SUITABILITY.

All tents are usually categorised by classifying them into suitable seasons of use and how many people they are designed to sleep. Season ratings might also be replaced with description of areas and levels of camping they are suitable for. Some examples include:

Summer season, or one to two season = Valley tents. (Sheltered).

Two to three season = Mountain tents. (Exposed to harsher weather).

Four season = Able to withstand harsh winter weather. (Heavy snow fall and particularly strong winds).

Five seasons = for places that offer worse than British winters.

Occasionally different manufacturers construct their own, more detailed, methods of rating and measuring the strength of their designs.

Obviously a tent described as a "two man tent", is suitable for use by two people. Sometimes they may fall at the edge of a category, (e.g. 2-3 man tent) so they might become, for example, a spacious two man tent, or an intimate three person tent.

Tents

An approximate weight guide:

(Relating to quality two-man versions)

Valley tents; 1.9kg to 4kg.

Mountain tents; 2kg to 4kg.

Four season; 3.5kg to 5kg.

SHAPES AND DESIGNS.

RIDGE TENTS: The definitive and classic tent shape is the traditional run of the mill ridge tent design. Two upright poles support a single ridge pole from either end. This creates the typical oblong ground shape, with triangular upright end shapes. Occasionally you may dispense with the ridge pole, relying on the end guy line's tension pulling apart the two uprights to support the tent. This will reduce the pack weight but reduce the tent's strength.

This design still serves for many but increasingly more common only on basic budget tents.

Sloping ridge tents still use two uprights but feature one noticeably shorter than the other. This reduces the weight and pack bulk of the overall tent but drastically reduces internal space at one end. Mostly popular with one man tents, but with two-man versions, the inhabitants need to sleep head to head, as the sloping ridge pole only leaves the necessary head room at one end.

Battling off modern alternative tent concepts, sloping ridges can still produce many of the lightest and smallest pack sized tents available, often with relative price advantages.

Transverse ridge tents follow the basic ridge tent design, but are wide enough to allow inhabitants to sleep across the tent, rather than lengthwise; usually creating a squarer ground shape. This has the advantage of allowing two occupants to sit and simultaneously enjoy the maximum height of the tent directly from their sleeping position. Plus, a tent with squarer ground shape, or lower height relative to its ground area, improves stability. Typically, transverse tents feature two bell ends.

(Bell ends to follow). With two man tents this provides each man with his own storage area conveniently to his side.

"A" framed tents, use two poles, joined at the top, creating an "A" shape (or inverted "V") replacing singular upright poles. (Some sloping ridge tents may feature a single "A" frame at the entrance) This vastly improves the tent's strength and is particularly popular for extreme expedition use. (It also allows improved ease of access, as the entrance isn't impeded by a central upright).

Some tents allow "A" frames to be added separately, allowing a choice for various occasions. Lighter standard uprights for summer, or heavier, but stronger "A" frames for winter.

"This one's particulary resistant to harsh wind."

"Oh good, I suffer terribly from that."

The following tents all offer more space for less/equal weight.

DOME TENTS: As the name suggests, these are tents in the shape of a dome. Thin flexible poles curved and held under tension create numerous aerodynamic shapes, usually improving user ergonomics, and often increasing stability and reliability. The simplified design logic: Tents that dance with the wind, rather than stand and fight.

Tents

Popular advantages include; Vastly improved living comfort, as extra head room is created and spread over a larger area. No concerns about pitching into the wind, as it's aerodynamic from all angles. Is free standing, so if necessary, on a rocky pitch, it may be weighted down with boulders. Due to its free standing design it may easily be moved, carried and relocated, while still erected. Is easier to pitch single handed.

There are two types; Square domes (two poles crossing) and hexagonal domes. (Three poles crossing).

Square domes, aren't as stable as their hexagonal relatives but still provide improved ease of erection and added head room. Comfortable valley tents and usually cater for economy budgets.

Hexagonal domes, provide the added strength necessary for mountain use. As the better dome tents usually prefer this design, hexagonal (or three pole) domes usually feature many advantages. (e.g, bell ends, flysheet first, alloy poles, etc. Details to follow)

SINGLE HOOPED TENTS: The name accurately describes the design; a single hooped (curved) pole supporting the tent that splays out from it. These can follow the basic design of traditional ridge tent lay outs, or transverse ridge designs. Best suited as particularly lightweight backpacking tents for modest use (valleys), but often have limitations with storage space.

TUNNEL TENTS: Rather than one single hoop these tents use two or more to create a tunnel effect. (For lightweight backpacking, usually only two). Often each hoop is a different height and size to create a lighter or more stable variations.

Basic tunnel tents can be vulnerable to side winds. They are usually a little too heavy for true backpacking use, but serve well as tents to return to each evening, or as easy-pitching conveniences for sight-seeing car travellers.

GEODESIC TENTS: Similar to dome tents, these provide improved strengths due to the improved physics of interacting hoops which cross at several points. (i.e, no single point where all poles cross). Four to six pole designs are much stronger than three pole versions, often providing the strongest structures for mountain use, but are also amongst the heaviest.

There are many variations of geodesic designs, but common on four season versions are valances. (Extra flaps skirting the bottom edge of the tent = helps deflect winds and allows additional rocks and boulders to weigh the tent down. Some four season "A" frame ridge tents may also have valances..

SINGLE OR DOUBLE SKIN

Years ago all tents were single skinned, made from a single layer of cotton which on contact with rain, the fibres expanded blocking its holes, and as a result tightened, increasing its surface tension, providing a perfectly watertight shelter. However, ever touched the underside of a wet umbrella? As with cotton tents, this breaks the surface tension and quickly allows water to ingress.

Due to other advantages covered in the following "Materials" section, proofed nylon avoids this and is the most popular choice of tent fabric today, but unfortunately, unlike cotton, doesn't breathe. Due to our breath reacting with the cooler outside nightime temperatures, such tent fabrics quickly suffer from internal condensation. Double skinned tents, using an inner and an outer tent (or flysheet), are the solution. This creates an air barrier or gap diluting the difference in air temperatures, which reduces the condensation rate and creates an air flow, removing much of the moisture vapour. The inner tent also catches and stops moisture from dripping back inside the main compartment.

You can avoid both cotton and double skinned tents by using a lightweight, waterproof, but also breathable fabric. See "Breathable single skinned tents" in the "Materials" section

INNER OR OUTER FIRST

With double skin tents, for typical British weather, it makes sense to have a tent that allows the waterproof outer to be pitched first. So that in wet weather, the inner tent doesn't get wet when pitching or striking camp. It also provides the quickest shelter for the occupier, allowing the inner to be erected from within.

Tents

Tents that can be erected inner tent first, are good in hot and dry climates, allowing the user to sleep with only the cooler inner erected, providing protection from mosquitoes, etc.

MATERIALS.

Flysheet; Cotton provides weather-tight protection, breathes, is tough and, if looked after, can last decades, but when wet is heavy, takes a fair while to dry and if stored damp, easily develops mildew. (Cotton contracts when wet, so guy lines should be slackened before retiring, in case it should rain during the night. This is the opposite to nylon).

Modern proofed nylons (occasionally polyester*) are obviously lighter, smaller packing, faster drying, but also suffer from their own disadvantages. However, due to the major advantages they do offer, they remain supremely popular.

(*Polyester flysheets stretch less than nylon when wet).

To make nylon waterproof it's usually proofed with polyurethane (PU), which offers admirable service for most tents, but some elite models opt for silicone elastomer coatings. PU coatings (and others) are applied in a molten state which heat ages the nylon and reduces the tear strength. Silicone elastomer provides a much greater tear strength. (The differences of waterproofing levels and UV resistance is negligible).

Nylon degrades and weakens with exposure to the sun's ultra violet light, but many quality proofed nylons now incorporate UV inhibitors which reduce the problem. (Nylon 66 is the most naturally resistant form).

The better nylon fabrics are proofed on both sides. This prevents the outer side absorbing moisture. Most fabrics will have a light water resistant silicone protection on the outside, but this will need to be regularly re-applied.

Inner tents; Traditionally, lightweight cotton was universally preferred for inner tent use, as it breathed and was considered cooler. The better type (sometimes polycotton mixtures), should be proofed = dry quicker, are mildew and rot resistant and stop sudden movements of the flysheet from dropping moisture droplets back inside the tent.

Coinciding with a demand for ever lighter tents, it's generally been found that extremely lightweight, lightly proofed, nylon fabrics also provide an equally adequate job, for a fraction of the weight.

Ripstop nylon is often used, in different weights, for both inner and outer tent fabrics. See "Sleeping bags chapter" page 122.

Breathable single skinned tents; are usually made from Gore-tex. (For full details see page 53) A tent made from a waterproof but also breathable fabric, allows a tent to be produced with only a single layer, but without the disadvantage of single layered cotton or nylon.

Advantages include; Faster and easier pitching and striking as there is no inner tent. More internal space. Fully and quality taped seams. Far higher waterproof levels.

Disadvantages include; They're not cheap! Also due to the physics of how breathables work, the one possible disadvantage is condensation or clamminess when used in warm climates, and/or condensation caused by a reduction of internal warmth. e.g occupants inside sleeping bags. The fabric's Nexus lining helps absorb moisture to dissipate later and avoid any drops of moisture forming.

Phoenix (committed manufacturer of G.T.X tents) use second generation Gore-tex, which has no problems with contamination, etc, (Details; see bottom of page 54) and offers a similar life span to conventional tents.

Groundsheets; If you're sensible, groundsheet fabrics needn't be as bomb proof as most people seem to think. Under normal use, tent weight can safely and drastically be reduced. A typical modern example is a standard 4oz proofed nylon. (Some versions use a Neoprene coating = for it's weight is extremely tough, but occasionally can crack in sub-zero temperatures). Lighterweight nylon groundsheets exist for extreme weight savings. Heavy weight PVC coated versions are certainly durable, but only found on expedition designs, or larger communal tents and are heavy!

(Some quality manufacturers offer a groundsheet replacement service).

SEAMS.

Stitching; Some manufacturers may take the trouble to bar tack seams at stress points, which certainly gives strength, but in time can weaken a fabric. Others may boast overlock safety stitching, or rolled seams. Zig-zag stitching at key points is particularly durable as it spreads tension over a larger area of the fabric.

Cotton flysheets should use the correct needles and thread. The cotton thread should swell sufficiently when wet to block it's own holes.

Waterproofs; Seams on nylon flysheets should ideally be doped, especially on mountain or four season models. (See the "Care" section)

Some manufacturers use taped seams (as found on waterproof clothing) and consider it the logical modern solution to sealing seams, but with many of the cheaper versions, the finish and eventual results aren't satisfactory. After a season's use, and particularly with inner tents suspended directly from a flysheet seams, the taping is often found to leak and poses a difficult job for the user to reseal. In most instances, weighing up cost and durability against the effectiveness of D.I.Y sealing, it's considered, in the long run, better ignored.

However, with the handful of true quality tent manufacturers, who go to the trouble and expense of taping seams properly on suitable tents, it is truly an advantage. (e.g Suspension points are eventually taped a third time, in between layers of stitching. But the heat from taping can weaken nylon).

POLES.

With traditional straight, or nesting poles, some steel versions are still available, but most now use the weaker, but far lighter, alloy alternatives.

Flexible poles (as used on all dome, tunnel, single hoop and geodesic tents) are certainly lighter. Plastic (or fibre glass) is light and cheap, but are likley to eventually become brittle and snap, particularly in cold temperatures,. Quality tents prefer the use of high tensile flexible alloy. Such poles are likely to set after a while (maintain a slight curve) but this won't affect performance and efforts to re-straighten them are pointless.

All the best poles are shock corded. This is a durable elastic cord that runs through the entire length of a set of poles, which avoids losing any, eliminates confusion, but most of all greatly accelerates the speed of assembly. Simply shake the poles out and they should lock themselves together.

Designs of how and where the end sections fit to the tent vary considerably. Webbing pockets are strongest but eyelets for pole spikes are easiest. Putting these poles in their sockets, etc, gets easier with use, but it can be a genuine problem especially when poles are wet. (Some shops may allow you to have an in-store trial run). The sleeves, or tunnels, for poles are easiest when uninterrupted = without any gaps.

Anodised poles are corrosion resistant, but due to the added expense are now reasonably rare.

BELL ENDS.

These are areas, on most tents, designed for equipment storage, or partial shelter for cooking. (Surplus space encased by the flysheets also incorporating entrances). The variations are endless and should be considered as a major feature for consideration. In my experience, most tents win or lose according to their bell end designs. A particular favourite - two separate bell ends, in a hexagonal dome tent.

POINTS IN GENERAL.

Colour: These days tents are available in many bright and wonderful colours, but it might be worthy of note that some camp-sites offer reduced camp fees for more subdued colours (greens, browns) and there are some that won't even allow bright colours.

Midges, etc, love yellow inner tents. Choose more subdued colours for less attention.

Brightly coloured guy lines are a good idea. We all know the problems of walking around a camp-site after dark.

Zips on doors should be double ended. By partially opening the top end you create a chimney effect and help reduce condensation.

Coiled zips are usually self repairing if you should burst one.

Mosquito nets are now a common and useful feature. Usually with tents that have zipped inner doors, they provide a second zipped opening that allows full ventilation but protection from undesirables. Handy for sleeping in warm weather.

Some tents are designed to allow you to pitch and strike the inner and outer tent together. (Never unclipping them apart). This can speed proceedings up, but when taking the tent down, condensation from the inside of the outer usually wets the inner tent, making it harder to dry and much heavier. (Normally you would shake off surplus moisture from the flysheet seperately).

Self Erecting tents; There is a recent resurgence in self erecting tents. (Tents permanently attached to a collapsing frame, which uses a number of lockable joints). They have been around before, including inflatables, but can rarely be considered for serious backpacking use. While they work perfectly well and are certainly quick to erect, due to their necessary construction they are somewhat heavier than equivalent tents of equal size and price.

CARE

Alloy poles don't rust but can corrode. To increase their life, wipe them dry after use. (Avoid salt water and rinse down after camping in sea breezes). A straightened skewer peg inserted inside and bound with tape around the outside, can make an adequate field repair should any poles kink, or snap. With flexible poles, push out through sleeves rather than pull.

With pegs, scrape off mud (damp mud will corrode) and place them in their bag, sharp end up, so not to pierce the bag's bottom.

Zips can be lubricated, e.g. run a candle along them.

Dope seams to seal them. There are many products available from camping shops, some in handy paint-on form. (Or use, Evostik, Bostik, Clear dope, or Loctite Clear. Avoid wax sealants). For best practical results apply to both sides, but this can tarnish the tents appearance, so most users find it perfectly adequate to seal just the inner side.

Many proofings on the flysheet's outer side fade after a while. If you find the outer absorbing blotches of water, reproof with any of the dozens of suitable sprays or brush on coatings available from camping shops.

If not already treated, the inner tent should also be proofed, for the reasons covered in the "Materials" section. Never cook inside the inner tent. Provide bell ends with plenty of ventilation when cooking.

It seems to miss the point some what, but many people take the precaution of providing an extra under-layer groundsheet, to protect the bottom of their tent from sharp stones, etc. Needless to say, when possible, always have a quick scout around for anything that may cause damage before pitching.

Never store tents damp. Even synthetic fabrics can suffer from mildew. You can halt the progress of mildew with a trip to the Chemist, treating the tent with a mild solution of Milton sterilising fluid. To avoid accelerated hydrolysis (resulting in coatings sticking together and breaking down) on proofed synthetics, when storing for long periods of time, sprinkle a little talcum powder, or climbers chalk, over the proofed side of fabrics.

If you have to, clean with mild soap and water. If necessary reproof. Dry and air thoroughly.

MANUFACTURERS.

The following is only a brief selection of some manufacturers of note:

Lichfield: Sound tents and excellent value for money, these British made tents provide a fine selection of most styles and designs.

Phoenix: Brilliant tent designers and manufacturers, with a tent for every occasion, from Welsh backpacking to Himalaya conquering. Many nylon double skins, but also champions of Gore-tex tents.

Robert Saunders: With a substantial history of innovations, these are amongst the best in the world for lightweight tents.

Vango: Still produce their traditional top quality and popular "Force Ten" range, but also provide modern designs and styles at prices less wounding to the pocket.

Other quality tents include: Wild Country, Vaude, Jack Wolfskin, Northface.